Confronting the spirit of religion

Ann Marie Alman

Confronting the spirit of religion
by Ann Marie Alman

Printed in the United States of America

ISBN 978-1-60647-078-7

www.xulonpress.com

Dedication
❧ ❦

This book is dedicated to all those in the body of Christ who are faithfully following Jesus and advancing the kingdom of heaven in the earth.

Contents

ᗏ ᘏ

Introduction

❧ ❧

17 "Do not think that I have come to abolish the Law or the Prophets; I have not come to abolish them but to fulfill them. 18 I tell you the truth, until heaven and earth disappear, not the smallest letter, not the least stroke of a pen; will by any means disappear from the Law until everything is accomplished.
Matthew 5:17-18

Jesus, the fulfillment of the Law

In the gospels, Jesus constantly confronted the religious groups – the Scribes, Pharisees and Sadducees. Why? They did not understand that Jesus came to fulfill the Law and not to confirm it. Also, when Jesus saw what had become of the Law, there was no doubt that He, being the One assigned to bring fulfillment, had to address it.

At the root of Jesus' concern were the Law of Moses and the way in which it was used as a tool of manipulation by the religious order for their benefit. The Law of Moses was a divinely instituted rule of life mediated through Moses to govern God's covenant people, Israel, in Canaan. It regulated their common, everyday conduct and was a covenant of works (Exodus 19:5-6). The Mosaic code of laws included the commandments (Exodus 20:1-17), the ordinances stipulating the Israelites' social life (21-23), and those directing Israel's worship (25-31).

It is this system; including the Ten Commandments as a way of life that Jesus came to bring to an end and to usher in a new system of grace. Grace replaced works. The Mosaic Law was a temporary divine administration in effect only until Christ should come. (Romans 5:13; Galatians 3:19).

However, the Pharisees taught such a strict obser-vance to the letter of the law that the true purpose of the Law was completely overlooked. The most amazing purpose of the Law was that it should have pointed to something higher than the letter. But because the Pharisees multiplied minute precepts and distinctions to such an extent, upon the pretense of maintaining it intact, the whole life of Israel was hemmed in and burdened on every side by instruc-tions so numerous and silly that the purpose of the law was almost, if not wholly, lost sight of (Matthew 12:1-13; 23:23-30).

Who are the Pharisees?

The name Pharisee means "separatists" and refers to a prominent sect of the Jews who carefully kept themselves from any legal contamination, distin-guishing themselves from the common people by their care in such matters. They held a stricter view of the concept of uncleanness; not only the uncleanness of the heathen but of all Israel.

As an Israelite avoided as far as possible all contact with a pagan, for fear of being defiled, so did the Pharisee avoid as far as possible *contact with the non-Pharisee*. The Pharisees were an exclusive religious group of Israelite. This seems to be the reason why they were called the separated or separating.

- o In the time of Jesus and the apostles, the Pharisees were a prominent sect of the Jews who had supreme influence over the people.
- o They were experts of the law (Mark 14: 3).
- o They were teachers of the law (Luke 15: 2).
- o They formed the strictest sect of the Jewish religion (Acts 26: 5).
- o They were members of the Sanhedrin (John 11: 47).

The Sanhedrin

Throughout the Gospels and the Book of Acts, the Sanhedrin is frequently mentioned as being the supreme Jewish court of justice (Matthew 5:22; 26:59; Mark 14:55; 15:1; Luke 22:66; Acts 4:15,21-23; 6:12-15; 22:30; 23:1,6; 24:20). The Sanhedrin was, above all, the final court of appeal for questions connected with the Mosaic law (Matthew 26:65; John 19:7; Acts 4).

The Sanhedrin council was made up of high priests (i.e., the acting high priest, those who had been high priests, and members of the privileged families from which the high priests were taken), elders (i.e., tribal and family heads of the people and priesthood), scribes (i.e., legal evaluators), Pharisees, and Sadducees (Matthew 26:3,57,59; Mark 14:53; 15:1; Luke 22:66; Acts 4:5-6; 5:21; 22:30Acts 4:1, 5:17,34). The number of members was seventy, with a president, a vice president, and servants of the court (John 18:22; Mark 14:65). Although the Sadducean high priests were at the head of the Sanhedrin, the Pharisees held the majority of seats on the council and consequently had the greater influence.

Most of Israel had a friendly disposition towards the Pharisees. They had the greatest influence upon the congregations, so that all acts of public worship, prayers, and sacrifices were performed according to their ruling. Although their number was comparatively small, they had absolute sway over the masses.

According to the Talmud (the body of Jewish civil and ceremonial law), there were seven kinds of Pharisee.

1. The Shechemite Pharisee, who simply kept the law for *what he could profit* from it.
2. The Humbling Pharisee, who so as to *appear* humble always hung down his head.
3. The Bleeding Pharisee, who in order *not to see a woman* walked with his eyes closed, and thus often met with wounds.

4. The Mortar Pharisee, who wore a mortar-shaped cap to cover his eyes that he *might not see any impurities or indecencies.*

5. The What-am-I-yet-to-do Pharisee, who, not knowing much about the law, as soon as he had done one thing, asked, "What is my duty now and I will do it" (Mark 10:17-22).

6. The Pharisee from Fear, who kept the law because he was afraid of future judgment.

7. The Pharisee from Love, who obeyed the Lord because he loved Him with all his heart.

It was obvious to Jesus that if the Pharisees missed the purpose for the Law, they would miss the Kingdom – *the new way of life mediated through Christ which the Law of Moses pointed to.* The Law was a guide on how to live but the Pharisees got stuck in the letter of the Law and missed the spirit. The purpose of the law was not to bring God's people into a tradition of mere rituals but rather to cause them by the Spirit to live life under the sovereign rule or will of God – the kingdom.

Under the influence of the Pharisees, true godliness lost its value and was neglected. Life with God that was meant to have its place in the heart vanished. What was left was a form of godliness void of the power of God. Relationship was reduced to rituals. This was not the purpose of God. Life with God does not consist of outward appearances but of substance. It is not about outward observances but inward spirit; not in small details, but in great principles of life.

The whole system of Pharisaic holiness led to exactly opposite conclusions.

Christ taught holiness as a spiritual reality but the Pharisees were able to "look" and "act" holy so that they could attract attention and gain the admiration of men. They prayed, fasted, fed the poor and gave solely to receive praise from man (Matthew 6:2-4, 16-18; 23:5-7; Luke 14:7-11; 18:11-14).

Everything that Christ represented as it pertains to the fulfillment of the law, the Pharisees managed to lose sight of due to their view of and strict adherence to the letter of the law. Christ had an immeasurable compassion for the dishonored and was helpful to the friendless. His liberality to the poor, holiness of heart, universal love, and open-mindedness to the truth was a direct contrast to the ways of the Pharisees.

The Pharisees regarded the dishonored classes of society as people to be avoided, not to be won over to the right (Luke 7:39; 15:2; 18:11), and pushed from them those that Jesus would have gathered within His fold. They made a prey of the friendless (Matthew 23:14) with their entire pretense to holiness. They were in reality greedy, fleshy, and self-indulgent (Matthew 23:25-28; John 8:7).

The Pharisees' teachings represented everything that was contrary to the way of life God intended for His people. They misrepresented God. Externally they appeared to be representing God but in reality they were products of their own ideologies.

In Matthew 23 Jesus and the Pharisees came to a head-on collision. His language was strong and without remorse. Jesus knew that the message and reality of the kingdom could not co-exist with the religious order– one canceled out the other. Jesus publicly exposed the demonic work of the Pharisees.

Today, though the Pharisees no longer exist, the spirit of the Pharisee is still ever present posing as the spirit of religion. We too must confront and expose this spirit in our lives, homes, ministries, businesses, and communities. This wicked spirit controls those that are controllable and stops them from enjoying the freedom that Christ has secured for them.

As Jesus laments over the Pharisees and Israel we see the characteristics and fruit of the spirit of religion. It is an extremely dangerous spirit and should be confronted every time it shows up. That was exactly how Jesus dealt with this spirit. We would do well if we follow His example.

Chapter One

The First Woe – Rejecting the kingdom of heaven
༉ ༉

"Woe to you, teachers of the law and Pharisees, you hypocrites! **_You shut the kingdom of heaven in men's faces._** *You yourselves do not enter, nor will you let those enter who are trying to.* Mathew 23: 13

The Religious Rejects the Kingdom of God

In addressing the religious order of the day, Jesus called the Pharisees hypocrites. A hypocrite is the same whether in Hebrew, Greek, or English. A hypocrite is one who acts a part; he takes on the part, acts the role perfectly but is not whom he says he is. He is one who pretends to be a Christian as he offers lip service to God. A hypocrite is one who hides behind the church so that he could carry out his own agenda. He puts up a façade. A hypocrite is a fraud.

As far as Jesus was concerned the Pharisees had no business being leaders over God's people. They had become such hypocrites that they forfeited any rights that they may have had to speak on behalf of God. They were hypocrites because they preached one thing but lived something else.

The religious spirit shuts the kingdom of heaven in men's faces. That is an insult! But it is how the spirit of religion works. The spirit of religion is not concerned about your freedom or salvation; it is a selfish and self-centered spirit. Its only concern is for what it believes and everyone else must either conform or be rejected.

Today, many people in our churches have not heard about the gospel of the kingdom – the central message of Christ. People have heard of every thing but the kingdom message. Others who have heard about the kingdom are still in a quandary about what it means. However, the real culprit behind the "mystery" of the kingdom is the spirit of religion. The goal of this wicked spirit is to stop you from experiencing the reality of the kingdom of heaven. And one way of doing this is to make the message of the kingdom so foggy, that people do not readily grasp it.

What is the kingdom of heaven?

First let us examine the word kingdom. Webster's dictionary describes a kingdom as a country, state or territory ruled by a king or queen. This speaks of a king and his domain. Therefore the kingdom of heaven is the rule, authority, or domain of heaven. Sometimes the Bible also speaks of the kingdom of

God. It is the same concept – the rule of God or the domain of God.

Therefore wherever the rule of heaven or of God is, the kingdom is. If God is ruler of your life then the kingdom has come to you. If God is the ruler of a family, ministry, business or country, then the kingdom has come to that family, ministry, business or country. Jesus taught His disciples to pray "Thy kingdom come, thy will be done on earth as it is in heaven." (Mathew 6)

The religious system stops you from experiencing the rule of God in your life because it has its own set of rules that it wants you to live by. If the religious system can get you to live all of your life following a bunch of rules, regulations, and rituals, it would have succeeded. The religious system works through systematic teachings and indoctrination and is very influential; do not underestimate it. Remember, the Pharisees were experts and teachers of the law. Teachers are very powerful people because they have the power to shape our belief system; they have the power to "set" our minds.

People who operate under a religious spirit suffer from a serious condition called know-it-all. They think that they know everything. That is a serious problem. Really, it is a control problem. A religious person seeks to control everything and everyone around him. Why? He knows everything.

Now, you know why the Pharisees, in spite of their expertise in matters pertaining to the law, completely missed Christ. They knew too much. Do you know anyone who seems to know everything? This person always has to let you know where he studied, how many degrees he has or how long he has been in the church. By doing that he is letting you know that he has seen everything and heard everything on a particular issue. There may be a heavy spirit of religion present in that person.

The spirit of control

Once, having been asked by the Pharisees when the kingdom of God would come, Jesus replied, "The kingdom of God does not come with your careful observation, 21 nor will people say, 'Here it is,' or 'There it is,' <u>because the kingdom of God is within you."</u>
Luke 17:20-21

The religious spirit loves to ask questions, debate, and discuss the kingdom but would seldom access it. This spirit is a spirit of control. The Pharisees expected the king of the Jews – Messiah, to come with fanfare, balloons, streamers, and trumpets. So when He was born of humble beginnings in a stable that was the beginning of their problems. God would not be controlled; He must always be in control. God must be free to do what He wants, when He wants, if He wants. Somehow, the Pharisees were unable to comprehend the freedom of God to do as He pleases. They thought that God was confined to a bunch of rules.

The Pharisees thought that the kingdom of heaven was another religious institution. *It is not.* It does not come with careful observation; *it is experiential.* The kingdom of God is within you; the rule of God is within you; the authority of God is within you. The kingdom of God is not a church or a denomination; it is a relationship with God through Christ.

The kingdom comes within the life of a person when the King comes into the life of that person. When the King comes the kingdom comes and when the kingdom comes the King comes. Wherever the King is in control that place becomes His domain. Therefore when anyone gives over the controls of his life to Christ, the kingdom of heaven becomes a reality in his life.

One of the problems we face in the church today is that many have come to the altar asking the King – Jesus, to come into their lives but have not relinquished control of their lives to the King. They still determine how they would live from day to day. *The only way to experience the kingdom is to give up control or else you would simply become a religious person.*

When a person invites the King into his life, he must surrender his desire to control his life and allow the King to rule him from the inside out. Now life is lived on the King's terms according to His word. That person has become the domain or sphere of influence belonging to the King – the kingdom has come experientially.

Once again, it is the religious spirit that is at work when a person comes to the altar, repeats all of the prayers but returns to business as usual - never experiencing God in a real way. This person can even start attending church regularly, sing regularly, give tithes and offering regularly but never experience the reality of God's rule in his life. This was the source of Jesus' pain with the Pharisees. They had substituted relationship for rules and rituals. God's people were following the rules but were not being drawn any closer to Him. The rules were set up to gain approval from and impress men; their traditions had little to do with God.

Nevertheless among the chief rulers also many believed on him; but because of the Pharisees they did not confess him, lest they should be put out of the synagogue: For they loved the praise of men more than the praise of God (John 12:42-43).

The whole pharisaical system was anti-Christ. The system literally stopped people from accessing God. That is the ultimate goal of the religious system – to stop you from coming to know God in a real way; to stop you from entering into a deep, personal, intimate relationship with Christ as King. Many people know Jesus as Savior, but not as king. It is to whom He is king that the kingdom comes. The leaders of the religious system do not enter the kingdom and they stop others from entering in.

The religious system believes that it is the answer to life's problems but *the Kingdom is the only answer to the chaos, calamity and challenges of our day.* In Eden, once Adam and Eve lived under the authority of God, all was well. The moment they established their own way of doing things, creation, including man, was plunged into bondage and decay (Genesis 3). Nebuchadnezzar's life was plunged into utter darkness because he thought that he was god. The moment he acknowledged heaven rules, he was restored to his place as king. He was a king but he was not *the* King.

Jesus came to earth to re-establish the authority of God in creation beginning with man. The kingdom of heaven or the reality of heaven is the only solution. A ritual is not the solution neither is a denomination. The only solution is Christ – the King and His domain.

In far too many churches the spirit of religion has been given a free reign and it's time to confront and cancel the work of this spirit. It manifests through leadership who controls every aspect of the worship of God's people. Everything is set like a program and must be followed even to the smallest detail. Sounds familiar! Yes, it is the same Pharisee spirit.

If God is not allowed to be in control then the spirit has once again successfully shut the kingdom of God in the faces of the people. The kingdom of God can only become a reality in a church setting when people relinquish control of the worship and allow Holy Spirit to take over.

I believe that we must pay special attention here because the kingdom finds expression within the context of the local church. It is experienced first in the life of a person (the kingdom is within you) and it spills over into the church, family, community and ultimately the whole earth. But what we have in a lot of churches is a religious expression and not a kingdom expression. Woe!

When men seek to control the church then there would be no manifestation of the kingdom of heaven. There would be no release of the gifts of the spirit – the religious resists the freedom of the spirit. There would be no miracles, signs or wonders. There would be no deliverances or casting out of demons. Jesus said, *"But if I drive out demons by the finger of God, then the kingdom of God has come to you."* Luke 11:20 The casting out of demons, healings, deliverances are all signs of the presence of the King – the kingdom of God. When God comes among a people He displays His power and we see signs and wonders.

1 Corinthians 12:7 says, "Each person is given something to do that shows who God is: Everyone gets in on it, everyone benefits. All kinds of things are handed out by the Spirit, and to all kinds of people!" (The Message) Some of these gifts that show who God is are word of wisdom, word of knowledge, faith, gifts of healing, working of miracles, prophecy, discerning of spirits, speaking in tongues, and inter-pretation of tongues. The spirit of religion would either shut down any display of God's power among His people or control any flow of the spirit. The goal is to shut out any manifestation of the King.

The religious opposes anything that is of the Spirit because it would mean that the Spirit is in control and would obviously get the glory; not man. It presents a fleshy and carnal gospel and keeps you from accessing the reality of the Spirit in your life.

Anyone used by this spirit would pick out parts of the scripture to justify his position and the person who does not have a working knowledge of the Word and a real relationship with God does not stand a chance around him.

Knowledge puffs up

Knowledge puffs up, but love builds up. 2 The man who thinks he knows something does not yet know as he ought to know. 1 Corinthians 8:1-3

A person who possesses great knowledge but lacks love is a dangerous person. The Pharisees were learned men but they did not love men enough to give them the freedom to choose to have God's authority in their lives. They opposed Jesus and His message of the kingdom every chance they got and used their great influence over the people to stop them from entering in.

The religious have this inflated sense of superiority. They are usually arrogant, feel superior and look down on others who are not as advanced as they are. The religious judges everything from the point of view of knowledge and never from the point of love. The Pharisees' sect was the product of their superior knowledge. They became the exclusive club in Israel who would only relate with those who were like them. That is a manifestation of the religious spirit – pride.

The religious never seek any further truth; "they know." Their minds are closed to any new thing that God is doing. They, by their superior knowledge, have managed to successfully box God out. He certainly cannot be boxed-in. Instead of seeking present truths, the religious would ask test questions to see if you know what you are talking about. Remember, when the religious ask a question, it is not because they want an answer. (Mathew 16: 1; 19: 3)

Their test questions usually surround contro-versial issues such as divorce, being filled with the Holy Spirit, speaking in tongues and whether or not a woman should hold any position of leadership in the church. Their goal is to trap you; not to gain any new insights or revelation. They also want to impress you by revealing how much they know about and can defend the particular issue.

The religious do not seek for new truths and they hinder others from doing so. This spirit blocks you from receiving spiritual truths. It will allow you read the daily newspapers, The Enquirer, Danielle Steele novels and so on. But a book loaded with spiritual truths that would help to unlock the truth of the kingdom in your life, would be a struggle. It would make you buy everything else but a tape or CD that will cause new levels of faith and faithfulness to be birth in you. *This is a hindering spirit.* Do not become a victim of the religious spirit; press in for present truths and seek the now-word of the Lord. No one knows it all.

Another way in which the spirit of religion stops you from receiving new truths is by providing special literature for those that belong to their denomination to read. Congregants are not allowed to read any literature from outside the denomination because everything and everyone else is in error. It is their way of controlling the minds of the people. The religious are afraid that the people may find out that they are being controlled and break free.

In some places, people are not encouraged to read the Word of God for themselves. Everything is prepared and read at the services. It is a religious spirit that hinders someone from personally seeking to know God through reading, studying, and meditating on His Word. As long as you follow rules and keep up with rituals you are giving the spirit of religion power to operate in your life. That way you will never experience God in a *real* way. What you will get is religion and not relationship with God.

When Jesus left there, the Pharisees and the teachers of the law began to oppose him fiercely and to besiege him with questions, 54 waiting to catch him in something he might say. Luke 11:53-54

The Pharisees heard the crowd whispering such things about him. Then the chief priests and the Pharisees sent temple guards to arrest him. John 7:32

The chief agenda of the religious spirit is to oppose and get rid of the revelation and manifestation of the kingdom of heaven. The religious system opposes

27

anything that is radical and represents change. The system takes pride in how it has not changed over the years. It is all about maintenance and not about advancement. The person who is under this spirit will remind you of their theological teaching and training. He would always refer to his tenure as a Christian. He believes that being in the church a long time qualifies him to speak on certain issues while he cites what he has seen and heard over the years. While we cannot deny years of experience in church affairs, we should never substitute present truths with past experiences. God is doing a new thing.

The Pharisees were the ones who studied the law. They would not access the kingdom themselves and they set up roadblocks for those who wanted to enter. They used their influence to stop the people from accessing the reality of the kingdom of heaven in their lives. Their knowledge literally stopped them from receiving and walking in the reality of the kingdom of heaven.

Chapter Two

The Second Woe – perverted apostolic ministry

ॐ ॐ

"Woe to you, teachers of the law and Pharisees, you hypocrites! You travel over land and sea to win a single convert, and when he becomes one, you make him twice as much a son of hell as you are. Matthew 23:15

The religious produce false sons.

The Pharisees were very careful to find new converts and would go great distances and spare no cost to win one. Their goal was to indoctrinate him and make him twice as much religious. They were actually practicing a five-fold ministry principle of raising spiritual sons for the work of the ministry. The portfolio really is that of the apostle being a fathering ministry. However, the religious does not produce sons of God, they produce *sons of hell.*

Those that are sons of the religious system are never plugged into God; they are plugged into their religious fathers, their dogmas and doctrines. They too do not know God experientially. These sons are not true sons because the religious fathers are hypocrites. They raise their sons to be hypocrites also – sons of bondage.

Religious fathers are not true fathers. True fathers never raise their sons to be just like them, making them clones. True fathers raise their sons to be everything God wants them to be. True fathers raise their sons on sound biblical principles and allow for difference.

Religious sons dress like their fathers, preach like their fathers, and live like their fathers.

Religion produces a counterfeit apostolic ministry but even worse than that, it produces a counterfeit church. It is not real; it is a fraudulent work. On the outside everything looks like church but on the inside the motive is corrupt.

This type of religious system is seen in Revelation chapter 3: 14 - 22.

"To the angel of the church in Laodicea write:

These are the words of the Amen, the faithful and true witness, the ruler of God's creation. 15 I know your deeds, that you are neither cold nor hot. I wish you were either one or the other! 16 So, because you are lukewarm — neither hot nor cold — I am about to spit you out of my mouth. 17 You say, 'I am rich; I have acquired wealth and do not need a thing.' But you do not realize that you are wretched, pitiful, poor, blind and naked. 18 I counsel you to buy from me gold refined in the fire, so you can become rich; and white clothes to wear, so you can cover your shameful nakedness; and salve to put on your eyes, so you can see.

19 Those whom I love I rebuke and discipline. So be earnest, and repent. 20 Here I am! I stand at the door and knock. If anyone hears my voice and opens the door, I will come in and eat with him, and he with me.

21 To him who overcomes, I will give the right to sit with me on my throne, just as I overcame and sat down with my Father on his throne. 22 He who has an ear, let him hear what the Spirit says to the churches."

The religious church has at its center money

The Laodicean church was a very powerful *religious* church. On the outside everything looked like church. They took great pride in their accumulation of wealth and self-sufficiency. But that was the problem. They needed nothing; not even Christ. They were too busy with their programs to even notice that Christ was not in the midst of them. Who needs Him anyway when you have all the money you could ever need? *The religious church is not centered on Christ; it is centered on money.* What a poor church!

The lukewarm church

This is a religious church because Jesus calls it lukewarm. Lukewarmness is a manifestation of the spirit of religion. A person that is cold knows he is cold. The person who is hot knows that he is hot. But the person who is lukewarm believes that he is alright and that sickens God. Doesn't that sound pharisaical? We have everything right. We have the buildings, the money, fine clothing and we know how to do church; we are not blind.

The Laodicean church was a church that had no impact on its community. Geographically, Laodicea was located between two other important cities, Colossae and Heiropolis. Colossae, wedged into a narrow valley in the shadow of towering mountains, was watered by icy streams which tumbled down from the heights. Heiropolis, was famous for its hot mineral springs which flowed out of the city and across a high plain until it cascaded down a cliff which faced Laodicea. By the time the water reached the valley floor, it was lukewarm, putrid, and nauseating.

At Colossae, one could be refreshed with clear, cold, invigorating drinking water. At Heiropolis, one could be healed by bathing in its hot, mineral-laden pools. But at Laodicea, the waters were neither hot (for health) nor cold (for drinking). In other words, the indictment against the church in Laodicea was that it was ineffectual – good for nothing. The church did not provide either refreshment for the spiritually weary or healing for the spiritually sick.

In order to address this church, Jesus sent a message of repentance to the principality over the church. In order to change the religious system of any church or denomination, the order of change has to start with the ruling angel over the church. The ruling spirit was the spirit of money. It is the spirit that must first be dealt with and in many churches today that struggle with religious manifestations.

Never underestimate the power of money. It can blind you and give you a false sense of security. It can make you start trusting in your physical appearance as the standard for righteousness. It can make you start believing that because you drive a certain car or live in a certain neighborhood that you are better-off or more important than those who may not be able to afford high-end cars or houses.

Wealth without the reality of Christ in your life will bring misery. The Laodicean church was wretched, pitiful, poor, blind, and naked. What an indictment against a church that was loaded with stuff! In the church, stuff is secondary; Christ is primary. Without Christ (not by name but by experience), the church is just a religious system that promotes death. It becomes a graveyard.

Religion produces a false church where Christ is just a name to be preached about but never a person to be experienced. The spirit of religion produces false churches where religious people go through rituals and traditions but never experience true fellowship with Christ because the door is shut in His face and He is kept on the outside. They have established programs specifically designed to keep Christ out.

The result is a church that does not affect its society; a church that has no transforming power. The church can only have power to impact its society if Christ is present but religion seeks to drive Christ out of the church.

How can one have fellowship with a Christ who is not present? The religious system offers you a Christ that is only accessible by special people. The common man must go through a series of channels through different rituals and traditions in his effort to access Christ. But Hebrew 4:16 tells us this: *Let us then approach the throne of grace with confidence, so that we may receive mercy and find grace to help us in our time of need.* And Hebrews 10:19-22 says, "*Therefore, brothers, since we have confidence to enter the Most Holy Place by the blood of Jesus, 20 by a new and living way opened for us through the curtain, that is, his body, 21 and since we have a great priest over the house of God, 22 let us draw near to God with a sincere heart in full assurance of faith, having our hearts sprinkled to cleanse us from a guilty conscience and having our bodies washed with pure water.*"

There is only one mediator between God and man. His name is Jesus Christ. No believer has to go through a saint or pastor in order to access God and God certainly does not need to go through anyone to have access to His people. Any system of worship that demand you pray to anything or anyone but Christ in order to access God is a fraudulent system. Do not engage in it.

The person with the religious spirit wants you to be connected to him more than you are connected to Christ. That way he can control and manipulate you. These types of fathers usually demand that you do nothing or go anywhere without their approval. They believe that God must first speak to them on your behalf before He speaks to you. Religious fathers teach their sons to be dependant on them and not upon Holy Spirit. Religious fathers plug their sons into them and not into the local church.

Revealing the sons of God

You are all sons of God through faith in Christ Jesus, for all of you who were baptized into Christ have clothed yourselves with Christ. Galatians 3:26-27 Every believer is a son of God. It is He who purchased our salvation and bought our freedom. God has adopted us into His family and made us His sons. We are joint-heirs with Christ. Never give that up! The spirit of religion is after your identity in God. Know whom you are and stay true to your King.

Interestingly, Romans 8: 19 – 21 says, *"The creation waits in eager expectation for **the sons of God** to be revealed. 20 For the creation was subjected to frustration, not by its own choice, but by the will of the one who subjected it, in hope 21 that the creation itself will be liberated from its bondage to decay and brought into the glorious freedom of the children of God."*

While creation is eagerly waiting for the sons of God to be revealed, religion produces sons of hell.

This is a deliberate plan of deception. Sons of God are sons filled with the purposes of God whereas sons of hell are filled with the plans of the wicked one.

Sons of God bring freedom

God's purpose for His sons is to bring freedom to the creation. Creation is in bondage and decay. The rule of God in the earth has been thwarted by the religious system and made ineffective. Man, having lost sight of God as the giver and sustainer of creation, has become enslaved by rituals and traditions of men. If man is in trouble, it stands to reason that the creation would be in trouble because man has authority over the earth. Man must be redeemed.

It is the redeemed man who is empowered to bring freedom to creation. Once again, the religious system seeks to intercept the plan of God, keeping man and ultimately the creation in bondage. Religion is a system that enslaves man seeking to stop him from accomplishing his ultimate purpose in the earth – to bring freedom to others and the whole of creation.

The creation is waiting for the sons of God to be revealed because creation wants to be liberated. Bondage leads to decay and creation knows it. The true sons of God are liberated; they walk in glorious freedom. That is why every believer needs to understand his relationship with God as Father. If He is Father then we are sons. As sons we have direct access to Him. Christ removed all of the barriers that once stopped us from accessing God. Let me show you a few things about sons of God.

o   Sons carry their father's name.
o   Sons carry their father's image and likeness.
o   Sons honor and respect their father.
o   Sons obey their father.
o   Sons receive discipline from their father.
o   Sons have legal rights to everything their father possess.

However, the spirit of religion produces sons of bondage, sons of decay; sons of hell.

Religion seeks far and wide to produce after its kind. It produces sons after its own image and likeness. It is constantly looking for people to indoctrinate into its religious program.

The religious program is a counterfeit program that opposes the plan of God to free creation. A person cannot give what he does not have. You cannot release freedom if you are tied up - hands, feet, heart, and mind. In order to bring freedom you must be free. The religious spirit is a spirit of bondage that produces sons of bondage – a misrepresentation of true apostolic ministry.

Beware of the yeast of the Pharisees

Meanwhile, when a crowd of many thousands had gathered, so that they were trampling on one another, Jesus began to speak first to his disciples, saying: "Be on your guard against the <u>yeast</u> of the Pharisees, which is hypocrisy. Luke 12:1

Jesus was very careful to warn His followers about the hypocrisy of the Pharisees. Today we too must take heed. The teachings of the religious agenda, like yeast, have the power to spread and eventually take over. When a little yeast is released into dough, with time it spreads throughout the whole dough (1 Corinthians 5: 6). That is the power of a little religious teaching. A little legalism here and there has the potential to bring bondage on one's life and ministry. We will deal with this some more in the section on legalism.

It is our duty to safeguard our lives from any such teachings orchestrated by the spirit of religion and allow Holy Spirit to teach us all things. John wrote in 1 John 2:26-27, I am writing these things to you about those who are trying to lead you astray. As for you, the anointing you received from him remains in you, and you do not need anyone to teach you. *But as his anointing teaches you about all things* and as that anointing is real, not counterfeit — just as it has taught you, remain in him.

John talks about a real anointing and a counterfeit anointing. The religious carry a counterfeit anointing and though the teachings sound deep and spiritual, we must be aware. It is our responsibility to hear from Holy Spirit on the teachings and interpretation of scripture, lest we follow patterns and interpretations that are purely religious. Religious teachings are hypocritical and when you examine their doctrines you will find many holes in them. The religious person talks from three sides of his mouth. He says one thing, means another and yet does something else. Our duty is to practice what we preach so that we do not facilitate the religious spirit and by our hypocrisy become fathers or sons of hell.

Before we move on, allow me to say this. We must take the time to examine the things handed down to us by our parents both natural and spiritual. Why? Because many of their beliefs may have come from a religious place and if that is so, these teachings should not be adopted. Also, we must be careful not to adopt the practices of our parents without first finding out for ourselves the reason why they did it. Because a thing sounds or looks spiritual does not mean that it is of Holy Spirit. It could be coming from a counterfeit anointing.

The story is told of a young lady who for most of her life saw her mother cutting off both sides of the roast when it was baking time. She eventually got married and started to do the same thing whenever she had to do a roast. Her husband challenged her. After trying unsuccessfully to convince him that it was necessary that she cut off both ends of the roast, she called her mother. Her mother explained that the only reason why she cut off both ends of the roast was because the pan was too small. Got it?

It is natural to model our parents and teachers. They are in our lives for a reason. However, we must seek to know Christ personally and allow Holy Spirit to teach us all things and guide us into all truth. If we do not, we will end up with our teachers and fathers replacing the role of Holy Spirit in our lives. And ultimately, that is the goal of the religious spirit. Do not let it happen to you.

Chapter Three

The Third Woe – wrong motives
୬ ୬

"Woe to you, blind guides! You say, 'If anyone swears by the temple, it means nothing; but if anyone swears by the gold of the temple, he is bound by his oath.' 17 You blind fools! Which is greater: the gold, or the temple that makes the gold sacred? 18 You also say, 'If anyone swears by the altar, it means nothing; but if anyone swears by the gift on it, he is bound by his oath.' 19 You blind men! Which is greater: the gift, or the altar that makes the gift sacred? Matthew 23:16-19

Blind Leaders

The first thing about this woe worth noting is that the guides are blind. To guide is to lead, steer or direct. Can you see the picture? The leaders who were supposed to be leading the people to God are blind. They are in darkness and therefore, have lost their ability to lead. The religious spirit disqualifies a leader from leading. It blinds him concerning the real reason for the law and it darkens his understanding of the truth (Matthew 22: 41-46).

The religious leader does not have the ability to lead because he is blind. He lacks insight into the things of God. He lacks true spiritual discernment. He sees only what he wants to see – he sees only what would benefit his carnality. This spirit is a selfish spirit and is only concerned about self. Even when this spirit does a good deed it is to gain the approval of men.

> *"Be careful not to do your 'acts of righ-teousness' before men, to be seen by them. If you do, you will have no reward from your Father in heaven.*
>
> *"So when you give to the needy, do not announce it with trumpets, as the hypocrites do in the synagogues and on the streets, to be honored by men. I tell you the truth, they have received their reward in full.*
>
> *But when you give to the needy, do not let your left hand know what your right hand is doing,*
>
> *So that your giving may be in secret. Then your Father, who sees what is done in secret, will reward you.* Matthew 6:1-4

Whatever the Scribes, and especially the Pharisees, did was usually done to gain man's approval. Followers of Jesus must do nothing to impress men but their lives must be governed by the **inward desire to be approved of God.** Living to please God must become a principle that we live by. Whatever we do must be done from the inside. Watch against hypocrisy.

Let's see why Jesus warned against being like the Scribes and Pharisees. They gave alms. The question was not their giving of alms or helping the needy; *it was their motive.* No one can see your motives. It is a matter of the heart. On the surface, everything looks kosher; it looks normal. Everything looks the way it is supposed to look because you are doing the right thing. But the heart no man could see; motives are difficult to see with the eyes. It is for this reason; we need to be careful concerning matters of the heart. Motives can be contaminated.

We need to constantly examine and guard our hearts from wrong motives. Always ask why before you do acts of righteousness; it will help to keep your heart in the right place. Ask questions like, "What do I hope to accomplish by doing this?" Some people give to a project or ministry with the hope of getting a promotion in the ministry or on a team. Others give to be seen by or gain access to the pastor or leader. Their motives are wrong. We need to always watch out for hypocrisy; it's a direct result of impure motives. Whatever you do, it must always be done to be approved of God and not of man.

So the Pharisees and the Scribes they gave alms and large sums of money to the treasury. Remember the Pharisee and the tax collector who went to the temple to pray? *The Pharisee stood up and prayed* about himself: *'God, I thank you that I am not like other men — robbers, evildoers, adulterers — or even like this tax collector. I fast twice a week and give a tenth of all I get.'* [Luke 18:10-12] To the Pharisee, everything he does is to get exalted; he is constantly seeking to get a higher position. It is all about him. He prayed about himself.

They gave their alms, but not from any principle of obedience to God or love to man or compassion to the poor. None of those things played any role in their giving. It wasn't because they wanted to be obedient to God. It wasn't because they loved the poor or had compassion on the poor. It was all about them. It was done so that they could get honor and be put in the high seat. And that they could get promoted so people could look at them. They gave but it wasn't from the heart. They gave to gain pride and vain glory. It was a big show. They gave so that they could be praised by men. Because their giving was so public, the public held them in high esteem. They gave to serve their own egos and desires.

Jesus calls this hypocrisy because the purpose of giving alms should be to bless the other person. But the Pharisee gave to bless himself. When a Scribe or Pharisee decided to do some alms giving at his house, he would make a loud sound with a trumpet pretending to call the poor. His reason, though, was to inform the surrounding neighbors of his intentions. He would announce it with trumpets, so that everyone in the neighborhood would be aware of the charity meeting at his house.

Jesus says when you give, be sincere and humble. Do not let your left hand know what your right hand is doing. Whenever you are giving alms, do it in secret; don't announce or proclaim it. Do it from your heart and your Father who sees what is done in secret, He will reward you openly.

The religious is blinded by gifts and gold

The religious spirit blinds those who are looking for attention. Wrong motives drive us to make wrong decisions. The religious – the Pharisees, taught that if you swore by the temple or the altar that your word was not binding but if you swore by the *gold* in the temple or the *gift* on the altar, then your word was binding. What a narrow view!

The spirit of religion has a narrow understanding of the things of God. It is very limited in its scope and depth. The revelation that comes from the spirit of religion is shallow and convenient. This spirit promotes money and materialism over the temple and the altar. In the religious setting, revelations are understood in terms of gold and gifts. It is usually why the leader ends up being blind. Gold and gifts have the power to blind you. The religious sacrifices the spiritual for the material. This spirit places way too much emphasis on material things rather than the spiritual purpose for them.

"No servant can serve two masters. Either he will hate the one and love the other, or he will be devoted to the one and despise

the other. You cannot serve both God and Money."

14 The Pharisees, <u>who loved money</u>, heard all this and were sneering at Jesus. 15 He said to them, "You are the ones who justify yourselves in the eyes of men, but God knows your hearts. What is highly valued among men is detestable in God's sight. Luke 16:13-15

The Pharisees loved money. They loved money and gifts. The love of money is the root of all evil and the person who does not have a clear understanding about the true purpose of money will end up serving it. In my book, "*Where are the servants,*" I dealt with the question of money and here is a quick overview.

o   Do not underestimate the power of money.
o   Money must honor God.
o   Money does not bring real satisfaction.
o   Money cannot buy peace.
o   Money cannot buy love.
o   Money cannot buy a good name.
o   Money cannot buy wisdom.
o   Money is transitory.
o   Money is a blessing.
o   Money is a tool to finance your vision.

The Pharisees' love of money corrupted their decisions. It short-circuited their ability to see clearly the true meaning of spiritual things. The religious spirit is very selective in its revelation. Whatever would benefit the flesh is what would be promoted. If you follow this spirit you will fall into a ditch.

The religious are masters of evasion

There is yet another side to Jesus' disapproval of the spiritual leaders of His day. Religion uses evasion to get its way and the Pharisees were masters of it.

"Again, you have heard that it was said to the people long ago, 'Do not break your oath, but keep the oaths you have made to the Lord.' 34 But I tell you, Do not swear at all: either by heaven, for it is God's throne; 35 or by the earth, for it is his footstool; or by Jerusalem, for it is the city of the Great King. 36 And do not swear by your head, for you cannot make even one hair white or black. 37 Simply let your 'Yes' be 'Yes,' and your 'No,' 'No'; anything beyond this comes from the evil one.
Matthew 5:33-37

In matters of oaths, the Jewish legalists were masters of evasion. To the Jew an oath was absolutely binding, *so long as it was a binding oath.* But what was a binding oath? A binding oath was an oath in which the name of God was used. Such an oath must be kept, no matter what the cost. Any other oath might be legitimately broken. The idea was that, if God's name was actually used, then God was introduced as a partner into the transaction, and to break the oath was not only to break faith with men but to insult God.

The Pharisees brought the science of evasion to a high point. They taught: if you swear by anything but the gold or the gift you can get out of it. The whole idea of treating oaths in this way is basic deceitfulness. *Why make a promise with the deliberate intention of evading it?* With regards to keeping their promises, the Pharisees would seek to get out on a technicality. Remember, they were the experts of the Law.

Moses said to the heads of the tribes of Israel: "This is what the LORD commands: 2 When a man makes a vow to the LORD or takes an oath to obligate himself by a pledge, he must not break his word but must do everything he said. Numbers 30:1-2

If you make a vow to the LORD your God, do not be slow to pay it, for the LORD your God will certainly demand it of you and you will be guilty of sin. 22 But if you refrain from making a vow, you will not be guilty. 23 Whatever your lips utter you must be sure to do, because you made your vow freely to the LORD your God with your own mouth. Deuteronomy 23:21-23

But by the time of Jesus, the Jews divided oaths into two classes; those which were absolutely binding and those which were not. Any oath which contained the name of God was absolutely binding; any oath which succeeded in evading the name of God was held not to be binding. The result was that if a man swore by the name of God in any form, he had to keep that oath but if he swore by heaven, or by earth, or by Jerusalem, or by his head, he was free to break that oath. The result was that evasion had been brought to a fine art.

Jesus addressed the issue by saying that no man can keep God out of any transaction. Heaven is God's throne; earth is His footstool; Jerusalem is the city of God and a man's head does not belong to him. He cannot even make a hair white or black; his life belongs to God. Everything in the world belongs to God and therefore, whether God is actually named in so many words or not, does not matter. God is there already.

The fact is that God does not need to be invited into certain departments of life, and kept out of others. He is everywhere, all through life and in every activity of life. He hears not only the words which are spoken in His name; He hears all words; and there cannot be any such thing as a form of words which evades bringing God into a transaction. We will regard all promises as sacred, if we remember that all promises are made in the presence of God. Therefore, we should say yes and nothing more; no and nothing more. But whether we say yes or no we should keep our promises.

The Pharisee spirit is a master at evasion. This person seeks to get out from his responsibilities by saying things like, "My season is over," or, "The

Lord says," or, "I have a right to." It is a matter of saying one thing but doing another. Remember, God hears every word we say and knows the motives of every heart. We must be true to our words.

Chapter Four

The Fourth Woe – legalism
ॐ ॐ

"Woe to you, teachers of the law and Pharisees, you hypocrites! You give a tenth of your spices — mint, dill and cumin. But you have neglected the more important matters of the law — justice, mercy and faithfulness. You should have practiced the latter, without neglecting the former. 24 You blind guides! You strain out a gnat but swallow a camel. Matthew 23:23-24

What is legalism?

Legalism is *excessive* adherence to the details of law. It is the use of the Law to enslave someone. Once again this is the religious spirit at its best – focusing on externals while the inner being is left to decay. The focus is usually on the small stuff while the weightier matters get overlooked. The religious go through all the rituals. They have the best chairs, building, equipments but the inner man is left to perish – immorality, pride, unforgiveness, hatred, malice, and strife just to name a few is left to run rampant.

Legalism focuses on the external – what you wear, what you eat, how you eat, what you drink, the building, the chair, and the décor, just to name a few. It seldom addresses your attitudes, your spirit, your temperament, or your character. *Legalism neglects the more important matters and emphasizes elementary stuff.* Legalism majors on minor issues and consequently misses the big picture. I believe that in our churches today, the spirit of legalism is the most dangerous and most common manifestation of the spirit of religion.

The tithe was an essential part of Jewish religious regulations. *Be sure to set aside a tenth of all that your fields produce each year* (Deuteronomy 14:22). *"A tithe of everything from the land, whether grain from the soil or fruit from the trees, belongs to the LORD; it is holy to the LORD"* (Leviticus 27:30). This tithe was especially for the support of the Levites, whose assignment was to do the material work of the Temple and the things which had to be tithe were defined by the Law.

Jesus' problem with the Pharisees was this. It was accepted that the tithes of the main crops must be given. But mint, dill and cumin are herbs of the kitchen garden and would not be grown in large quantities. A man would have only a little patch of them. All three were used in cooking, and dill and cumin had medicinal uses. To tithe them was to tithe a tiny crop, maybe not much more than the produce of one plant. Only those who were exceptionally meticulous would tithe the single plants of the kitchen garden.

That is precisely how the spirit of legalism operates. The Pharisees were so absolutely meticulous about tithing that they would tithe even one clump of mint; and yet these same men could be guilty of prejudice; could be hard, arrogant and cruel. These same men would go to any lengths to punish anyone who breaks the law showing no mercy and would make promises with the deliberate intention of not fulfilling them. It was not that tithing one clump of mint was wrong but that they paid more attention to it than to matters of justice and mercy.

The religious spirit still operates in the same way today. It cares more about rules than about people. Justice, mercy and faithfulness are qualities that pertain to how we treat with people. Let us look at some examples of the legalistic spirit at work.

Legalism and the hungry

At that time Jesus went through the grainfields on the Sabbath. His disciples were hungry and began to pick some heads of grain and eat them. 2 When the Pharisees saw this, they said to him, "Look! Your disciples are doing what is unlawful on the Sabbath." Matthew 12:1-2

The problem that the Scribes and Pharisees had with the disciples was not that they had picked and eaten grains of corn but that they did it on the Sabbath day. The Law stipulated that a man should not do any work on the Sabbath day. But the interpreters of the Law were not too happy with such a simple law; they had to complicate it so that it became difficult for others to do it.

From that one command the interpreters of the Law came up with thirty-nine basic actions that could not be performed on the Sabbath including reaping, winnowing and threshing. Also, meals could not be prepared on the Sabbath day. To eat on the Sabbath day, meals had to be prepared the day before. This was the disciples' crime. They prepared their food on the Sabbath day – they broke the Law.

Jesus responded to the religious order by reminding them of a time when David and his men were so hungry that they went into the tabernacle and ate the showbread which only the priest could eat. Interestingly, no blame was attached to them. Why? They were hungry. *Human need must take precedence over any ritual custom.* What the spirit of religion does not understand is that the Law points to a relationship with the Law-giver; it was not given to kill but to breathe life. As far as the Pharisees were concerned Jesus and His disciples could have died of hunger; they should have prepared their meals ahead of time. The Law is the Law and it must be kept at all cost regardless of the circumstances. The law is hard, cold and uncaring and so is the legalistic spirit.

In His defense, Jesus quoted the Sabbath work of the Temple. The priest had to kindle fires, slaughter and prepare animals, lift them on to the altar, and a host of other things. Any ordinary person who performed any of those actions on the Sabbath would have been guilty of breaking the Law. But for the priest it was perfectly legal to do work because the Temple worship must go on. Worship takes precedence over Sabbath rules and regulations. The legalists refused to accept Jesus' response and of course completely denied all the evidence that pointed to and exposed their legalism. The Pharisees were so bent on keeping every rule of the Law that they could show no mercy, which by the way is of greater significance to God.

Once, I was told by someone that if a person who was a Christian, had a smoking habit, he would go to hell. If a believer died immediately after committing _one_ act of sin that he was going to hell. I was shocked. But I understood what was at work. That is the Law at work; certainly not grace. In other words, there is no room for mercy or grace. You break the Law; you burn in hell seven times over. This is a classic example of the legalistic mind at work. It is cold and hard. Let us make a quick examination of this.

Salvation by Christ alone

It is clear that the wages of sin is death, but the gift of God is eternal life in Christ Jesus our Lord (Romans 6:23). Eternal life is found only in Christ and not in works. As a Christian you cannot do anything good enough to gain God's favor. It is what the Bible calls dead works, from which we must repent or change (Hebrews 6: 1-2). The legalist believes that you must work (hard) to get into heaven. So even if after you have accepted Christ and you struggle with a weakness or sin, you will go to hell. My friend, that is salvation based on works. In other words, one is saved based on his ability to deal with his problems. That is not the teaching of the scriptures.

James 2:10 says, *"For whoever keeps the whole law and yet stumbles at just one point is guilty of breaking all of it."* The truth is that no one can keep the Law of God. If we stumble in one point we are guilty of all points. There is nothing that we can do that will get us a place in heaven, no habit to break; *only* Christ can get us there. Anyone who practices salvation by works may be in danger of a more serious indictment – idolatry.

This person is actually putting himself in the position of savior – he is trying to save himself. This practice is seen in people that worship other gods. They constantly perform rituals in their efforts to appease their gods. The believer who trusts in his good works or good behavior to please God has been deceived by the devil in the same way as the idol worshipper.

We are accepted by God because of Christ *alone. For it is by grace you have been saved, through faith — and this not from yourselves, it is the gift of God— not by works, so that no one can boast.* Ephesians 2:8-10 We have favor with God because we have placed our trust in the person and work of Christ. It is not by works that we are saved. The word is very clear about this.

Paul, the apostle, rebuked the Galatian Christians who got deceived by a religious legalistic spirit.

Someone told them that after they were saved by faith that they had to *do things* to get into heaven. *You foolish Galatians! Who has bewitched you? Before your very eyes Jesus Christ was clearly portrayed as crucified. 2 I would like to learn just one thing from you: Did you receive the Spirit by observing the law, or by believing what you heard? 3 Are you so foolish? After beginning with the Spirit, <u>are you now trying to attain your goal by human effort?</u> 4 Have you suffered so much for nothing — if it really was for nothing? 5 Does God give you his Spirit and work miracles among you because you observe the law, or because you believe what you heard? Galatians 3:1-5*

A believer does not make it to heaven because he goes to church, reads his Bible, witness to unbelievers, and helps the poor, or give tithes and offerings. In churches that operate under the spirit of religion, people are taught to trust in their good works. For example, a person who has a smoking habit is made to feel that he is going to hell and certainly not accepted by God. How sad! God does not accept us because we have overcome a bad habit or addiction. He accepts us because Jesus Christ died on a cross over two thousand years ago. When we receive Him, we become His sons and daughters.

When we surrender our lives to Christ, He gives us the power and grace to stop or break any habit that is damaging to our person or does not glorify God *but He accepts us as we are and gives us the desire to change.* When we overcome an addiction it does not give us more favor with God, we already have His favor. God has called us to do good works but not to get us into heaven (Ephesians 2: 10). We do not do good works to become righteous; we do good works because we are righteous. The only way to heaven is through Christ (John 14: 6).

When a person accepts Christ, he must be careful not to add on all kinds of good works with hopes of becoming more righteous. God does not accept us because we read the Bible the right way, pray the right way, worship the right way, eat the right foods or dress the right way. Our acceptance is in Jesus Christ alone, period!

Knowing Christ and having an intimate relationship with Him is much more important than what we do or have done for Him. The legalistic spirit will rob you of a real relationship with Christ because you are never worthy; never righteous enough; always have to be doing something to gain favor with God.

The legalistic person preaches achieving right living as a way to heaven but Jesus teaches desiring right living as a kingdom way of life (Matthew 5: 6). This person may not achieve this righteousness in that he never makes a mistake, but he *longs for it with his whole heart*. If heaven was only for perfect people then no one would get there. *The true wonder of man is not that he is a sinner, but that even in his sin he wants to do right.*

Legalism and the blind

> *Therefore the Pharisees also asked him*
> *how he had received his sight. "He put mud*

on my eyes," the man replied, "and I washed, and now I see."

16 Some of the Pharisees said, "This man is not from God, for he does not keep the Sabbath." John 9:15-16

In this story, the Pharisees refused to accept Jesus as a man of God simply because He did not keep the Sabbath. Again, they failed to understand that God cares more about people than rules and regulation. In fact one of the purposes of the law is to bring man to God. Once man comes to God there is no longer any need for the Law (Galatians 3). The religious spirit could care less about your problem; the only thing that is important is the Law.

Imagine this young man, blind from his birth that never saw the light of day. Jesus healed him; his eyes were opened and for the first time this man was able to see anything. All the Pharisees cared about was that he was healed on the Sabbath. They would not celebrate with this man; their religion blinded them to real human needs, struggles and victories.

But there was a greater issue at hand – the issue of control. Jesus did not operate within the guidelines of the religious system. He refused to be conformed; He was a radical; words that the religious would label as rebellion The Pharisees could not control Jesus. He healed whenever He determined that a healing was necessary and ate when He was hungry. Jesus moved in a realm that the Pharisees could not control – the realm of the supernatural. Religious men would always seek to curtail the supernatural, limiting it to a set of rules or program. It is almost their way of trying to control God. But alas! God would not be controlled. He just moves on. Ichabod – the glory has departed.

Jewish tradition did not allow for healings on the Sabbath. Medical attention could be given only if life was in actual danger. Help was given only to keep the patient from getting worse, not to make him any better. For example, if a man's hand or foot was dislocated he may not pour cold water over it. Clearly the man who was born blind was in no danger of his life; therefore Jesus broke the Sabbath when He healed him.

The Pharisees are typical of the people in every generation who condemn anyone whose idea of religion is not theirs. *They thought that theirs was the only way of serving God.* Although some of them thought otherwise and declared that no one who did the things Jesus did could be a sinner, as a sect they struggled. Clearly, Jesus is demonstrating the power of God while He seems to be breaking all the rules. How could this be? The legalistic spirit will see the evidence but still hang on to its old beliefs. This person has closed his mind to present truths. For the legalist, serving God is about keeping rules and not about real love for God.

Jesus uses a gnat and a camel to illustrate the hypocrisy of the Pharisees. A gnat was an insect and therefore unclean; and so was a camel. In order to avoid the risk of drinking anything unclean, wine was strained through muslin gauze so that any possible impurity might be strained *out* of it. This was a very funny picture which must have made those listening laugh, of a man carefully straining his wine through gauze to avoid swallowing a microscopic insect and yet cheerfully swallowing a camel. It is the picture of a man who has completely lost his sense of balance.

The legalistic spirit majors on the minor. They are very meticulous on matters of the law but neglect the weightier issues of the Law. Some of the issues that the religious system has allowed to bring division in the church are the Sabbath and the supernatural as in the validity of speaking in tongues, the ministry of healing and deliverance. These are only the tip of the iceberg of issues that the legalistic mind focuses on while neglecting matters of mercy and justice.

In Paul's day, the church was embroiled in matters about special days, meat, drink (wine – to drink or not to drink), special clothes, circumcision and a whole host of other issues. We will see how Paul handled the churches then because we can learn how we should handle these types of issues as we face them today. In order to show how the spirit of religion works today, I will address the issue of wine drinking. My goal is not to convince any person or group one way or another (that is for each person to decide based on the word) but to simply point out how the spirit of legalism works and how we should deal with it.

We must be able to identify and confront this spirit. It usually wraps itself in deductions from the Word and mingles with personal conviction. If this spirit finds its way into a person who is influential – its person of choice - it can then promote new laws that followers must adhere to. Once a new law is introduced, most people immediately follow it without really consulting with Holy Spirit. The spirit of legalism has won. The truth is that there is a natural trust that students have for their teacher.

For example, if a leader says to his congregation that going to the movies is a sin, members of that congregation immediately would either not go to the movies or the ones that do go, would do so believing that they are sinning. That is the amount of power a teacher of the Word has over a congregation.

What is so sad about this issue is that most leaders who still hold a view against movie going do so based on the past culture surrounding movie going. In fact, during the early days Christians were warned against watching television when it was first introduced. Leaders, labeled watching TV as a sin. Today, almost every home has at least one television set, including the homes of most of those leaders who were adamantly preaching against it. "The law" against watching TV has become obsolete.

In fact, the very thing that was once labeled "of the devil" is now an evangelistic tool in the hand of the church to reach millions of people across the world. Personally, I believe that it is the responsibility of every child of God to choose what programs he should look at. He should make his decisions based on his relationship with God and not based on rules. The same principle applies to going to the movies.

Since there is no law that says believers should not go to the movies, leaders can provide counsel and alert their followers of the potential dangers of watching movies with certain content, but to pass a law prohibiting members from going to the movies or labeling it as a sin is to enter the realm of heavy legalism.

What is the key to understanding how we deal with certain issues in the church? If the matter is one that jeopardizes salvation then there is no compromise but if it doesn't then we must allow for difference. Let us look at the question of wine drinking and see what we can understand about the spirit of legalism.

Legalism and wine drinking

Is wine drinking a sin? There are many who believe that it is and there are many others who believe it is not. There are many references to wine and wine drinking in the Bible but none of the passages point to the drinking of wine as a sin. If fact, at least on one occasion in the New Testament wine drinking was recommended. But the scriptures are clear that we must be very cautious in this area and even spells out some of the negative results that can occur when wine is *abused*.

As we look at this issue we must bear in mind two groups of people – the liberals, who hold a wide view on matters and the conservatives, who hold a narrow view on matters with little room for choice. The spirit of legalism likes the conservatives. They see the law but would not see mercy.

One argument put forward by the conservative group is that wine drinking in the Old Testament was permitted but in the New Testament we should not drink real wine. We should operate in the "spirit" of wine. Usually, Ephesians 5: 18 is quoted which says, *Do not get drunk on wine, which leads to debauchery. Instead, be filled with the Spirit.* Now, the Bible did not say to not drink wine; it says *do not get drunk.* The argument put forth is that the only way to get drunk is to drink, so do not drink. Here comes the secondary law and this is the problem.

To not drink because one does not want to get drunk is a personal conviction and decision; one that every believer is free to make. However, the person who makes the decision to not drink wine or alcohol must also realize that *a person can drink wine and not get drunk.* When someone makes his conviction a universal law then he has made a new law. It is what the scribes (the interpreters of the law) did.

God said that no work should be done on the Sabbath and the interpreters of the law interpreted work to mean a person could not light fire, carry wood, lift a pot and so could not cook on the Sabbath day. In fact, they made thirty-nine laws that defined work; all this from one command; no wonder Jesus did not limit His ministry to the interpretation of the Scribes and Pharisees Sounds radical? Absolutely!

How is it that Jesus broke the Sabbath – He clearly did, but did not sin? 1 Peter 2:21-22 says, *"To this you were called, because Christ suffered for you, leaving you an example that you should follow in his steps. "He committed no sin, and no deceit was found in his mouth.""* Hebrews 4:15 says, *"For we do not have a high priest who is unable to sympa-*

thize with our weaknesses, but we have one who has been tempted in every way, just as we are — yet <u>was without sin</u>."

You may be surprised to find out that a lot of what is considered sin is not, simply because it is based on human interpretation and not based on what God has said. When a teacher of the word says that drinking wine or alcohol is a sin, he is saying that based on *his* interpretation of the word and his conviction. Nowhere in the word is there a command against wine drinking. However, the Bible is clear about the dangers of *abusing* wine or alcohol. What are we really dealing with? What is the issue at hand? Is it the drinking of wine itself or the abuse of wine?

Let us look again at the KJV rendering of Ephesians 5:18. And be not drunk with wine, *wherein is <u>excess</u>*; but be filled with the Spirit. Excess is the power word. A person can only get drunk on anything if he drinks more than he should; if he drinks in "excess." Webster defines excess as a going beyond what is regarded as customary or proper; immoderate indulgence; intemperance in eating, drinking, etc; more than or above what is necessary, usual, or specified; extra.

A person does not drink wine for a belly-full as he would eat food. He drinks wine either for medicinal, celebratory, or covenantal reasons. When Paul said, "Be filled with the spirit," he was also making another statement: do not be filled with wine. To be "filled" with wine would be excessive.

This scripture should not be used in trying to make a case against wine drinking because it clearly would be a misinterpretation of the passage. The scriptures were not meant to have personal interpretations or else we would have chaos. The word of God is clear and we should not read into it. It says, do not get drunk.

Personally, I believe that it is the abuse of wine or excessive use of wine that is at the heart of this matter. This scripture is talking about over-indulgence, gluttony. Excessive use of wine leads to drunkenness. The abuse of wine leads to drunkenness. *It is drunkenness that is a sin; not the drinking of wine.* 1 Corinthians 6: 10; Galatians 5: 21; Ephesians 5: 18 Legalism however, pays attention to wine drinking itself but ignores gluttony and over-indulgence – the weightier matters.

What is wine?

Before we go any further let us take a quick look at wine. Wine is the fermented juice of grapes, made in many varieties, such as red, white, sweet, dry, still, and sparkling, for use as a beverage, in cooking, in religious rites, etc., and usually having an alcoholic content of 14 percent or less. Wine is also the juice, fermented or unfermented, of various other fruits or plants, used as a beverage or sauce, for example *gooseberry wine; currant wine.*

This is very important for us to understand because when the legalistic mind talks about wine he is really referring to strong drink and its effects. However, legalism blinds him to some wines and other beverages with little alcoholic content – these are banned also. In fact, if you drink anything with *any* alcohol you are sinning. Welcome to the world of legalism!

Wine in the Bible

According to Easton's Bible Dictionary, the common Hebrew word for wine is *yayin*, from a root meaning "to boil up," "to be in a ferment." Others derive it from a root meaning "to tread out," and hence the juice of the grape trodden out. The Greek word for wine is *oinos*, and the Latin *vinun*. But besides this common Hebrew word, there are several others which are thus rendered.

(1.) *'Asis*, "sweet wine," or "new wine," the product of the same year (Songs of Solomon 8:2; Isaiah 49:26; Joel 1:5; 3:18; Amos 9:13), from a root meaning "to tread," hence juice trodden out or pressed out, thus referring to the method by which the juice is obtained. *The power of intoxication is ascribed to it.* (italics added)

(2.) *Hemer*, Deuteronomy 32:14 (rendered "blood of the grape") Isaiah 27:2 ("red wine"), Ezra 6:9; 7:22; Daniel 5:1,2,4. This word conveys the idea of "foaming," as in the process of fermentation, or when poured out. It is derived from the root *hamar*, meaning "to boil up," and also "to be red," from the idea of boiling or becoming inflamed.

(3.) *Mesekh*, properly a mixture of wine and water with spices that increase its stimulating properties (Isaiah 5:22). Ps 75:8, "The wine [*yayin*] is red; it is full of mixture [*mesekh*];" Proverbs 23:30, "mixed wine;" Isaiah 65:11, "drink offering" (R.V., "mingled wine").

(4.) *Tirosh*, properly "must," translated "wine" (Deuteronomy 28:51); "new wine" (Proverbs 3:10); "sweet wine" (Micah 6:15; R.V., "vintage"). This Hebrew word has been traced to a root meaning "to take possession of" and hence it is supposed that *tirosh* is so designated because in intoxicating it takes possession of the brain. Among the blessings promised to Esau (Genesis 27:28) mention is made of "plenty of corn and tirosh." Palestine is called "a land of corn and tirosh" (Deuteronomy 33:28; comp. Isa 36:17). See also Deuteronomy 28:51; 2 Chronicles 32:28; Joel 2:19; Hosea 4:11, ("wine [*yayin*] and new wine [*tirosh*] take away the heart").

(5.) *Shekar*, "strong drink," any intoxicating liquor; from a root meaning "to drink deeply," "to be drunken", a generic term applied to all fermented liquors, however obtained. Numbers 28:7, "strong wine" (R.V., "strong drink"). It is sometimes distinguished from wine, c.g., Leviticus 10:9, "Do not drink wine [*yayin*] nor strong drink [*shekar*];" Numbers 6:3; Judges 13:4,7; Isaiah 28:7 (in all these places rendered "strong drink"). Translated "strong drink" also in <u>Isaiah 5:11; 24:9; 29:9; 56:12; Proverbs 20:1; 31:6; Micah 2:11</u>.

(6.) *Mesek*, "a mixture," mixed or spiced wine, not diluted with water, but mixed with drugs and spices to increase its strength, or, as some think, mingled with the lees by being shaken (<u>Psalms 75:8; Proverbs 23:30</u>).

In <u>Acts 2:13</u> the word *gleukos*, rendered "new wine," denotes properly "sweet wine." It must have been intoxicating. In addition to wine the Hebrews also made use of what they called *debash*, which was obtained by boiling down must to one-half or one-third of its original bulk. In <u>Genesis 43:11</u> this word is rendered "honey." It was a kind of syrup, and is called by the Arabs at the present day dibs. This word occurs in the phrase "a land flowing with milk and honey" (*debash*), <u>Exodus 3:8,17; 13:5; 33:3; Leviticus 20:24; Numbers 13:27</u>.

The effects of wine

Proverbs 20:1 says *Wine is a mocker and beer a brawler; whoever is led astray by them is not wise.* Let us look at it. Wine is a mocker. Who is a mocker? One of the meanings of mock is to deceive. It means that wine is deceptive. If you ever had wine before, you may understand this more quickly than someone who never had a drink or two of wine.

The effect of wine is deceptive. While drinking, you feel okay until you stand up. It is only then, that you realize you have had too much to drink. That is the deception. It creeps up on you. That is why proverbs 23: 30 tells us to not *linger* over wine. If a person is going to drink wine he must decide the amount that he is going to have and do just that. Do not sit at the table and just drink and drink and drink; it is a mocker; it is deceptive. But does it say do not drink. It does not. In fact a person can understand this scripture to mean that wine drinking is permissible as long as you do not get deceived by it.

Beer is a brawler. What does that mean? The King James Version says strong drink is raging. Again, brawling here is referring to the effects of strong drinks. Beer is considered a strong drink. Bear in mind, that in Palestine, this is a type of alcoholic beverage that was considered strong drink. Today, in some cultures beer is not considered a strong drink.

Whatever is considered strong drink, the one thing we know is that the effects are furious. It is not deceptive as wine; it is fast and furious. What did the Word say? Did it say do not drink them? No! It says, do not be led astray or deceived by them. It is unwise. Even if a person is led astray he has not sinned, he is unwise. He has made a bad decision to drink too much. That bad decision can lead him to commit sin but drinking in itself is not sin.

Jesus and wine

If drinking wine in itself is a sin then that would mean Jesus was a sinner and we know that is not true. Jesus drank wine. Jesus made wine. The spirit of legalism refuses to acknowledge this. Their revelation is that to put wine or any alcoholic beverage into the body is to put another spirit into ones body. Well, what did Jesus do? Did He put other spirits into His Body? Why did He turn water into wine? Not only did He turn water into wine but He did so at a time in the wedding when the guests already had too much to drink.

> *Jesus said to the servants, "Fill the jars with water"; so they filled them to the brim.*
>
> *8 Then he told them, "Now draw some out and take it to the master of the banquet."*
>
> *They did so, 9 and the master of the banquet tasted the water that had been turned into wine. He did not realize where it had come from, though the servants who had drawn the water knew. Then he called the bridegroom aside 10 and said, "Everyone brings out the choice wine first and then the cheaper wine <u>after the guests have had too much to drink</u>; but you have saved the best till now."*
>
> *11 This, the first of his miraculous signs, Jesus performed at Cana in Galilee. He thus revealed his glory, and his disciples put their faith in him.* John 2:7-11

The spirit of legalism would preach about this miracle but would still say that drinking wine is a sin. This wedding was a real wedding, with real people, real wine and a real Jesus in attendance. The wine that Jesus miraculously brought about was labeled the best. That is aged wine or what we would call vintage wine. This is no grape juice. Did Jesus perform a miracle so that people can commit sin?

Then we must examine the fact that Jesus was labeled a wine-bibber or drunkard. Matthew 11:18-19 says, *"For John came neither eating nor drinking, and they say, 'He has a demon.' 19 The Son of Man came eating and drinking, and they say, 'Here is a glutton and a drunkard, a friend of tax collectors and "sinners." ' But wisdom is proved right by her actions.""*

Jesus is referring to the accusations of the scribes and Pharisees of His day. He was called a drunk. I am in no way agreeing with the religious order of the day who took every opportunity to level serious charges against Jesus so as to discredit Him. Unlike John who ate no bread and drank no wine, Jesus ate bread and drank wine with others. He drank wine but He was not a drunk.

Again, Jesus drank alcohol; it was not grape juice. If it was, the Pharisees would not have labeled Him a wine-bibber. Once again that is the mind of the Pharisee – a legalistic person. If a person drinks wine, he is immediately labeled a drunk. Wine bibbers are those who drink too much wine (addicts) and we are warned to not associate with them (Proverbs 23: 20). Again, the emphasis is on "too much" and not drinking itself.

Jesus and Sweet wine

Some Christians today, in their efforts to "protect" Jesus claim that the wine Jesus drank was "sweet wine." This sweet wine is referred to as a non-alcoholic wine. While the religious in Jesus' day totally rejected Him (calling Him a drunkard), the Pharisee spirit today seeks to defend Jesus' actions by saying the wine Jesus drank was non-alcoholic; grape juice. However, a quick look at the scriptures reveals a different picture.

In Palestine the vintage takes place in September, and is celebrated with great rejoicing. The ripe fruit was gathered in baskets (Jeremiah 6:9), as represented in Egyptian paintings, and was carried to the wine-press. It was then placed in the upper one of the two vats or receptacles of which the winepress was formed, and was subjected to the process of "treading." Nehemiah 13:15; Job 24:11; Isaiah 16:10; Jeremiah 25:30; 48:33; Amos 9:13; Revelation 19:15. A certain amount of juice exuded from the ripe fruit from its own pressure before treading commenced. This appears to have been kept separate from the rest of the juice, and to have formed the "sweet wine" noticed in Acts 2:13. (Smith's Bible Dictionary)

In Acts 2:13 the word translated new wine is *gleukous*. This word properly means the juice of the grape which distils before any pressure is applied, and called must. It was sweet wine, and hence, the word in Greek meaning "sweet" was given to it. The ancients, it is said, had the art of preserving their new wine with the special flavor before fermentation for a considerable time, and were in the habit of drinking it in the morning. The contents after this process, were found to remain unchanged for a year, and hence the name *aei gleukos* - always sweet. (From Barnes Notes)

The legalistic mind, in its effort to justify Jesus' wine drinking, claims that this is the wine Jesus drank. The new wine or sweet wine is claimed to be without alcohol as it was preserved before the fermentation process began. However, the apostles, on the day of Pentecost were accused of being drunk with new wine. *But others made a joke of it and derisively said, They are simply drunk and full of sweet [intoxicating] wine.* Acts 2:13 AMP

Sweet wine is alcoholic

How could the disciples be drunk with wine that had no alcohol? How could they be drunk with grape juice? New wine is wine that has not aged hence the term "new." Let me explain what happens. The moment juice is extracted from the grapes, fermentation begins. At this early stage the alcohol content may be slight but if a person drank enough, he could get drunk. *The point is that alcohol is present.* In Palestine, what the ancients sought to preserve was not the non-alcoholic content of grape juice but the fresh flavor and sweetness of the juice. The process was said to have affected the extent of the fermentation process. The sweet wine maintained its flavor but *was alcoholic.*

Awake, you drunkards, and weep; wail, all you drinkers of wine, because of the [fresh]

sweet juice [of the grape], for it is cut off and removed from your mouth. Joel 1:5 AMP

Clearly, the elders in Joel's day became drunk-ards off the sweet juice of the grape (sweet wine), so much so that the Lord had to stop the flow of sweet wine. Again, God is not against sweet wine but he is against drunkenness. In Amos 9:13 the Lord prom-ised a steady flow of sweet wine. *Behold, the days are coming, says the Lord, that the plowman shall overtake the reaper, and the treader of grapes him who sows the seed; and the mountains shall drop sweet wine and all the hills shall melt [that is, every-thing heretofore barren and unfruitful shall overflow with spiritual blessing]. AMP [Leviticus 26:5; Joel 3:18.]*

In that day the mountains will drip new wine, and the hills will flow with milk; all the ravines of Judah will run with water. A foun-tain will flow out of the LORD's house and will water the valley of acacias. Joel 3:18

God prospered Israel with wine for Israel to enjoy; not for Israel to abuse it. Wine is never taken for a belly-full; it is taken to celebrate the blessings of God. Once wine was being abused, God cuts off the supply. God is against abuse and not His children partaking of His blessings. Excess and gluttony are the real issues here.

> *And I will make those who oppress you consume themselves [in mutually destructive wars], thus eating their own flesh; and they will be drunk with their own blood, <u>as with sweet wine</u>; and all flesh will know [with a knowledge grounded in personal experience] that I, the Lord, am your Savior and your Redeemer, the Mighty One of Jacob.* Isaiah 49:26 AMP

Sweet wine is intoxicating. It may not be labeled strong wine but it is intoxicating. It is much the same as it is today. There were different grades of wines then just as there are different grades of wines today. With some wines, because of the alcohol content it may take a longer time for a person to get drunk. Whether Jesus drank sweet wine, new wine, or just wine, the point is He drank alcohol.

The question of putting other spirits in a person's body when he drinks alcohol is not substantiated by scripture as being a sinful act. No person in the body of Christ can be more perfect than Christ. Today, the religious, in his view against wine drinking is making some heavy claims against Christ, just as the Pharisees did. The person who holds that kind of mind-set is doing today what the Pharisees did – calling Jesus a sinner and a drunkard. Be careful!

A person should make the determination whether he should drink wine or not. He should never be forced to drink wine. It is not a sin to drink wine and a person does not sin if he refuses to drink wine. We need to pay attention to the effects of excessiveness, gluttony, and addiction and let our lives be governed by Holy Spirit.

Leaders and wine

> *If anyone wants to provide leadership in the church, good! 2 but there are preconditions: a leader must be well-thought-of, committed to his wife, cool and collected, accessible, and hospitable. He must know what he's talking about, 3 <u>not be over-fond of wine</u>, not pushy but gentle, not thin-skinned, not money-hungry.* 1 Timothy 3:1-3 The message.

One criterion for leadership in the church is that a person must not be given to wine - <u>*mee paroinon*</u>. This word not only signifies one who is inordinately attached (addicted) to wine, a winebibber or tippler, but also one who is imperious, abusive, insolent, whether through wine or otherwise. (From Adams Clarke commentary)

This seems to give some room for wine drinking but any person who becomes addicted to alcohol is disqualified from being a leader in the body of Christ. It is clear that wine drinking is permissible. However, one can see why a person may want to take the position of drinking only non-alcoholic beverages. It is a very safe place. But does that make the person who takes a glass of wine or any other alcoholic beverage a drunk or a sinner?

Paul recommends wine drinking

And don't worry too much about what the critics will say. Go ahead and drink a little wine, for instance; it's good for your digestion, good medicine for what ails you. 1 Timothy 5:23 The message

Paul, the apostle is counseling his spiritual son Timothy on how he should conduct ministry and uses the opportunity to give him some personal advice. What was his advice to this young pastor? *Drink a little wine!* Paul knew that the critics will come out swinging left and right against this counsel but advised his son anyway. Paul understood and obviously believed that wine was good for digestion and had medicinal properties.

He obviously, did not believe that it was a sin and that anyone would go to hell if he drank wine or else he would not ask Timothy to compromise his salvation for some comfort. He did not believe that when a person drinks wine that he was putting another spirit into his body or else he would not recommend that Timothy do so. Jesus did not believe that either.

The legalist makes a bottle of wine look like the devil when the truth is that the devil is not in the bottle but in the man who has no self-control. By saying that when a person drinks wine he is putting another spirit into his body, the legalistic person is saying that *wine is a demonic substance.* Remember the Good Samaritan? He traveled with wine. In fact, he became the Good Samaritan because he had wine and oil on his person. The wine was use to help the man who got beaten and robbed heal from his wounds (Luke 10: 34). By the way, the religious, passed this dying man on the streets and never even attempted to help him.

The question that is begging to be asked is this: is it okay to use wine (a demonic substance) on the body? Is it okay to take cold medicine or any medication that contains alcohol? Is it okay to use wine for cooking? Is it that anyone who does drink alcohol whether it be in wine or medicine will be putting another spirit into his body? As far as the legalistic person is concerned the answer is yes and that person becomes a prime candidate for deliverance.

Legalism is a dangerous spirit. It makes one rule to cover another and then has exceptions that break its own rules. It is so confusing that the person caught in such a web has little chance of escape. Jesus warned His disciple to be aware of legalism. It takes away a person's attention from what really matters. In this case the important issue is substance abuse. Legalism focuses on the substance itself.

The church and wine

When you come together, it is not the Lord's Supper you eat, 21 for as you eat, each of you goes ahead without waiting for anybody else. One remains hungry, another gets drunk. 22 Don't you have homes to eat and drink in? Or do you despise the church of God and humiliate those who have nothing? What shall I say

*to you? Shall I praise you for this? Certainly
not!* 1 Corinthians 11:20-22

In Bible days it was the regular custom for
groups of people to meet together for meals. There
was a certain kind of feast called an *eranos* to which
each participant brought his own share of the food,
and in which all the contributions were pooled to
make a common meal. The early Church had such
a custom - a feast called the *Agape* or Love Feast.
All the believers would bring whatever food they
could to it, the resources were pooled and they sat
down to a common meal. It was a way of producing
and nourishing real Christian fellowship. At the love
feast food included wine.

But in the Church at Corinth, the love feast
had gotten out of control. What was the problem?
In the Church there were rich and poor; there were
those who could bring plenty, and there were slaves
who could bring hardly anything at all. Some in the
church had a problem with *sharing*. The rich did not
share their food but ate it in little exclusive groups by
themselves, hurrying through it in case they had to
share, while the poor had next to nothing.

The result was that the meal at which the social
differences between members of the Church should
have been non-existent only succeeded in aggra-
vating them. Paul rebukes this. The ancient world
was so divided; there were the free men and the
slaves; there were the Greeks and the barbarians—
the people who did not speak Greek; there were the
Jews and the Gentiles; there were the Roman citizens

and the lesser breeds without the law; there were the cultured and the ignorant.

The early Church is the one place where these barriers should not exist. The Church is the one place where all men could and did come together. At the Lord's Supper the selfishness of race and class was forgotten and a new basis for society found love of God in men for whom Christ died. A church where social and class distinctions exist is no true church at all. A real church is a body of men and women united to each other because all are united to Christ.

The Lord's Supper

The Corinthian church ate The Lord's Supper. What we do today is a far cry from any kind of food much more supper. It is misleading. In fact, we must admit that what we call The Lord's Supper in most of our churches is simply not true. Once again, the spirit of religion has reduced a powerful relational experience to a ritual and we bought into it lock, stock, and barrel. We must repent!

For the Greek, supper was the main meal of the day. When we say The Lord's Supper, we are not even talking about a meal. But the Greek word is *deipnon*. For the Greek the breakfast was a meal where all that was eaten was a little bread dipped in wine; the midday meal was eaten anywhere, even on the street or in a city square; the *deipnon* was the main meal of the day, where people sat down with no sense of hurry and not only satisfied their hunger *but lingered long together*. The very word shows that *the Christian meal ought to be a main meal where people linger long in each other's company.*

The problem with the Corinthians was that those who brought food to the meeting ate and drank without waiting for everyone. While some were full and drunk others had nothing to eat or drink. The church drank wine; it was a staple at dinner and even at breakfast. Paul did not rebuke the church for drinking wine and getting drunk; he rebuked them for not waiting for each other and not sharing with each other.

Once again, the drunk among them was a clear sign of one person having too much while another goes without. What is the problem? Too much! The problem is not eating or drinking wine; the problem is greed, gluttony. The true Christian cannot bear to have too much while others have too little; he finds his greatest privilege not in jealously guarding his privileges but in giving them away.

> *So then, my brothers, when you come together to eat, **wait for each other**. 34 If anyone is hungry, he should eat at home, so that when you meet together it may not result in judgment.* 1 Corinthians 11:33-34

Clearly, the church came together to eat, not the *Eucharist* but real food. That meal included bread and wine. Jesus ate with His disciples at Passover. His meal included lamb and vegetables - a real meal. It included bread and wine. Today, the church must abandon the religious Eucharist and get back to eating real food together - lamb, ham and jam. The bottom line is that we come together as a new society in Christ sharing lives together – eating, drinking, and lingering in each other's company. That is the true essence of communion.

Nelson's Bible Dictionary gives us a list of some of the uses of wine. Let us take a brief look at it.

Uses of Wine

Wine was a significant trade item in Palestine.

Solomon offered Hiram 20,000 baths of wine in exchange for timber (2 Chronicles 2:10,15). Damascus was a market for the "wine of Helbon" (Ezekiel 27:18). Fines were sometimes paid with wine (Amos 2:8).

Wine was used in worship.

Libations to false gods were condemned (Deuteronomy 32:27-38; Isaiah 57:6; 65:11; Jerimiah 7:18; 19:13), but the drink offering prescribed by the Law of Moses was a libation of wine offered to the Lord. The daily offering (Exodus 29:40; Numbers 28:7), the offering of the firstfruits (Leviticus 23:13), the burnt offering, and the freewill offering (Numbers 15:4) required one-fourth of a hin of wine. The sacrifice of a ram was accompanied by a hin of wine (Numbers 15:6-7). In the temple organization set up by David, Levites were appointed to supervise these wine offerings (1 Chronicles 9:29).

Wine was used as a common beverage, or drink, in Palestine.

A part of the daily fare of the Hebrew people, **wine was a creation of the Lord to cheer the hearts of men.** *Psalm 104:14-15 says, He makes grass grow for the cattle, and plants for man to cultivate — bringing forth food from the earth: 15 <u>wine that gladdens the heart of man</u>, oil to make his face shine, and bread that sustains his heart.*

Wine is a gift given to man by God and not Baal, as the idol worshipper thought.

She has not acknowledged that <u>I was the one</u> who gave her the grain, <u>the new wine</u> and oil, who lavished on her the silver and gold — which they used for Baal. 9 "Therefore I will take away my grain when it ripens, and <u>my new wine</u> when it is ready. I will take back my wool and my linen, intended to cover her nakedness. Hosea 2:8-9

o   Wisdom is said to have mixed her wine (<u>Proverbs 9:2</u>) in furnishing her table.
o   Wine might be drunk with milk (<u>Songs of Solomon 5:1</u>).
o   Melchizedek brought wine and bread to Abraham when Abraham returned from battle (<u>Genesis 14:18</u>).
o   Wine was offered by the old man of Gibeah to the traveling Levite (<u>Judges 19:19</u>).

o   Jesse sent David with bread, a skin of wine, and a young goat as a present when Saul was fighting the Philistines (1 Samuel 16:20).

o   Abigail brought David two skins of wine (1 Samuel 25:18).

o   The tribes of Issachar, Zebulun, and Naphtali brought wine to David (1 Chronicles 12:40) when David was made king.

o   Ziba brought David wine as he fled from Absalom (2 Samuel 16:1-2).

o   Job's children were drinking wine at their brother's house when disaster struck (Job 1:13,18).

o   Wine was on the list of supplies that the Persians furnished the captive Hebrew people when they returned to Jerusalem (Ezra 6:9; 7:22).

These are but a few of the many references to the use of *wine as food* among the Hebrew people.

Wine was used as medicine.

It was said to revive the faint. *The king asked Ziba, "Why have you brought these?"*

Ziba answered, "The donkeys are for the king's household to ride on, the bread and fruit are for the men to eat, and the wine is to refresh those who become exhausted in the desert." 2 Samuel 16:2

o Wine was suitable as a sedative for people in distress (<u>Proverbs 31:6</u>).
o Mixed with a drug, it was used to ease suffering (<u>Matthew 27:34; Mark 15:23</u>).
o The Samaritan poured oil and wine on the wounds of the injured traveler (<u>Luke 10:34</u>).
o The apostle Paul charged Timothy, "No longer drink only water, but use a little wine for your stomach's sake" (<u>1 Timothy 5:23</u>).

Misuses of Wine

The dangers of drunkenness are abundantly recognized in the Bible (<u>Proverbs 20:1; 23:29-35</u>).

o Wine often enslaved the heart (<u>Hosea 4:11</u>).
o The prophets accused Israel of being over-come with wine (<u>Isaiah 28:1</u>), of drinking wine by bowlfuls (<u>Amos 6:6</u>), and of wanting prophets who spoke of wine (<u>Micah 2:11</u>).
o Leaders were interested in drinking and were not concerned about the ruin of the country (<u>Isaiah 5:11-12; 22:13</u>).

The list of those drunken with wine in the Bible begins with Noah and includes Lot, Nabal, and Ammon (<u>Genesis 9:21; 1 Samuel 25:36-37; 2 Samuel 13:28</u>).

In the Bible wine is figurative of many things such as the blood of Christ (<u>Matthew 26:27-29</u>); the bless-ings of the gospel (<u>Proverbs 9:2,5; Isaiah 25:6; 55:1</u>); the exhilarating effect of the Holy Spirit's fullness

(Ephesians 5:18); of the wrath and judgments of God (Psalms 60:3; 75:8; Jeremiah 13:12-14; 25:15-18); the abominations of the apostasy (Revelation 17:2; 18:3); and of violence (Proverbs 4:17). As teachers of the word, we teach from the figurative perspective on wine but we should not deny the reality of wine. Wine was a basic commodity in biblical times and still is today in many cultures.

The necessity of sound teaching

Two things are behind the teaching that wine drinking is a sin and any other legalistic teaching in the church. The first thing is fear. Many leaders are afraid that many in their congregation would go out and start drinking, get drunk and commit sin. But the real fear is that they will lose their grip on the people. The purpose of fear is to stop freedom. Fear and freedom cannot live in the same house. Leaders must learn to trust in the absolute power of God and not pervert the word of God for their own benefit - to control people.

A leader does not have to make his own laws so that people can live right. The only way people live right is when they live according to the word of God; not some man made law. That is not right living. Holy Spirit is more than able to make the child of God live for God. A leader's job is to teach, preach, and give sound counsel; it is not to make universal laws. God is the only law-giver.

The hypocrisy of legalism

It is amazing that money, sex, power and food all have the same damaging effects when abused but no one is saying that a person should not have money, sex, power or food. Again, this was what Jesus confronted in the Pharisees – the hypocrisy; the double standard.

Legalism and money

Money is addictive; the love of it is evil. Ecclesiastes 5:10 says, *"Whoever loves money never has money enough; whoever loves wealth is never satisfied with his income. This too is meaningless."* How do you know that a person is addicted to money? He speaks about money all the time. He is overly excited with the potential of having millions or he is depressed when he has little to none; he becomes consumed with worry. Many who worry about the damaging effects of alcohol play down the havoc that the lack of integrity as it pertains to money is having in families, society, and the church.

Money is the number one cause of divorce in America. Not only is it the number one cause of divorce; it is on the top of the list of reasons for the fall of ministers in the church today. We should be more concerned about money in the church rather than wine drinking. Very little caution if any is preached in many of our churches when the issue of money is addressed.

Again, what we have are two extremes. One side believes that God's desire for His children is that they prosper and that includes money while the other side has taken the position that too much money corrupts and has basically taken a vow of poverty. These saints have allowed the dangers of too much to scare them into having little or none. The two positions are correct in principle – God wants us to prosper; money corrupts. How we flesh it out is another story. What is needed here is sound teaching that leads to proper understanding of financial prosperity and character development.

God warned Israel over and over again about having the proper attitude towards wealth (Deuteronomy 8). God blessed them and brought them into a wealthy place. Deuteronomy 8:18 *But you shall [earnestly]* **remember** *the Lord your God, for it is* **He** *who gives you power to get wealth, that He may establish His covenant which He swore to your fathers, as it is this day.* AMP

God is admonishing Israel to not forget but to remember. Why? Wealth can lead to amnesia. Having too much can cause a person to forget. This I have personally seen.

But in faithful Israel and in the Kingdom, wealth leads to *remembering, naming and referencing the God who makes life possible as creator.*

Having financial prosperity can be a challenge. Israel is warned even further in Deuteronomy 31:20. *For when I have brought them into the land which I swore to their fathers, a land flowing with milk and honey, and they have eaten and filled themselves* **and**

become fat, *then they will turn to other gods and serve them, and despise and scorn Me and break My covenant.* AMP

God's concern here is not about the good blessings that He would give to His people – it is His delight to do so. But it is about Israel becoming self-indulgent. God is concerned about excessiveness – the ultimate abuse. Israel would grow fat – satiation pushed to extreme self-indulgence. Too much wealth can lead to a turning away from the Creator who is no longer blessed or remembered and "*a turn to other gods.*" Too much wealth can lead to the violation of Gods covenant of generosity and gratitude. This turn in the church usually leads to bondage and loss of ministry.

This is not a book about money but what we must ask ourselves is how much is too much. The Bible promises prosperity but issues so many warnings about too much. Once again, too much is relative. What may be too much for one person may not be for another. In the same way, one glass of wine may be one too much for one person but be quite okay for another.

How much money do you need to be satisfied? How much power, sex or cars? How many houses, how big? How much is enough? Are you satisfied? By now you should realize that the reality of satiation is found only in Yahweh and never in things or in people. If your wealth leads you away from God then that is a sin. If your wealth leads you to arrogance, greed, and a superiority-complex, you have sinned.

God intends for us to receive and be satisfied with His provisions. He created the world and everything in it for us to *enjoy* – something that so many Christians miss. Too many people reject God's wonderful earthly provisions for us and are literally dying to get to heaven. We either miss life on earth or we put life on hold waiting for things that are beyond our control to happen. The truth is that it is only the people who find difficulty in living on the earth want to escape to heaven. God created earth and all that is in it as a gift for man to enjoy.

The world is a gift from God to man that keeps on giving. Life is a gift from God to man. How sad it is that so many Christians do not enjoy life. The culprit is our theology. We were told that we must suffer through life and when we get to heaven there will be no more suffering. Somehow, that got translated into the idea that Christians must live boring, sour lives. In fact, there are some leaders in the church today that see any form of fun as sin. They are killjoys. Most Christians are waiting to get to heaven to live. Brothers and sisters, God wants us to live for Him in the earth not in heaven. In fact, Revelation 5:10 says, *You have made them to be a kingdom and priests to serve our God, and they will reign __on the earth__."*

Too much money or too little of it is not the problem; inappropriate use is. Jesus tells of how difficult it is for the rich to get into heaven but most messages today on money focuses on millions of it (Matthew 19: 24). Again in Luke 16:13-15, Jesus makes another negative comment to the Pharisees – those who loved money, *"No servant can serve* *two masters. Either he will hate the one and love the other, or he will be devoted to the one and despise the other. You cannot serve both God and Money." 14 <u>The Pharisees, who loved money</u>, heard all this and were sneering at Jesus. 15 He said to them, "You are the ones who justify yourselves in the eyes of men, but God knows your hearts. <u>**What is highly valued among men is detestable in God's sight.**</u>"*

This last part of Jesus' statement can be interpreted to mean that money (what is highly valued among men) is detestable to God. Could this text be interpreted to mean that God hates money? What a tragedy that would be. ***We should not simply group a particular activity as sin just because we are warned of the potential dangers of abuse.*** A person should be free to make the decision as to whether he should partake or participate in any activity based on his ability and conviction.

But godliness with contentment is great gain. 7 For we brought nothing into the world, and we can take nothing out of it. 8 But if we have food and clothing, we will be content with that. 9 <u>People who want to get rich fall into temptation and a trap and into many foolish and harmful desires that plunge men into ruin and destruction.</u> 1 Timothy 6:6-9

Again, the passage above is to show the cautions in the word as it pertains to getting rich. But does that mean God does not want us to be rich? God wants us to be wealthy so He puts warning signs on the road to financial prosperity. He wants us to arrive there safely. He wants us to watch out for the money trap and the harmful desires that come with having too much that can bring us down. Just ask some of our fallen soldiers and they may tell you. We are encouraged by the word to be content with food and clothing. In other words don't live your life to be rich; live a contented life. Learn how to be abased and abound.

Financial wealth comes with its own advantages and disadvantages. God as a loving Father gives us proper counsel and leaves us with the decision to choose. This ability to choose is what strengthens our relationship with our heavenly Father. He wants us to consult with Holy Spirit and depend on Him for every decision we make in life. That way we do not live for Him based on the law but based on His spirit's guide. Is having money a sin? No! But greed is; pride is and arrogance is. The abuse of money leads to sin and that is the problem; not money in itself.

Legalism and sex

Sex is addictive and the effects are damaging to society in much the same way as money. It is the number two cause of divorce in America and scandal in the church. Any leader, especially a male, who has made it through ministry without being accused of having an inappropriate relationship with some one of the opposite sex is in the minority. Today, we have to include leaders who are being caught with persons of the same sex.

There is a silent pandemic in the church and we have adopted the ostrich-in-the-sand policy. Church secretaries have become famous ladies-in-waiting. Young ladies in the church are being sexually victimized by leaders who are hardly ever challenged. These leaders have become a law unto themselves and they must be stopped. Local church members and leadership must rise up and confront this type of abuse in the church.

Countless families have been destroyed because of sexual abuse which results in adultery, pornography, rape, and incest. Today, with the internet easily accessible to most people, pornography has invaded modern society including the church as a plague. No one denies that partaking in pornography is addictive and potentially destructive; no one denies that rape and other forms of sexual abuse results from a perverted mindset; we all agree, but we do not preach that we should not have sex because of the potential danger that its abuse presents.

Legalism and power

Power is addictive. Many powerful men and women can testify of the adrenaline rush that it provides. Throughout the local church we hear of all kinds of leadership abuse. Leadership abuse is misuse of power. Many people in the Body of Christ are hurting today because of some form of abuse from their leaders. Many have left the local church totally disillusioned. The reason? Abuse of power! Is power sin? No! The abuse of power can lead to sin.

Legalism and food

Food is addictive. All kinds of studies show that the number one killer today is food. What we eat is killing us. Many are addicted to caffeine, sugar, carbohydrates and many other substances found in food. Obesity is one of the faster growing diseases in America. Yes, it is now a disease. Around almost every corner, there is an all-you-can-eat restaurant. *Gluttony is a sin.* Gluttony is excessive eating or drinking. Some people just eat and eat and eat. Because someone abuses food, do we say that eating food is a sin? No!

By now you should have gotten the message. The culprit here is not wine, sex, power or money; the crime is one of abuse; inappropriate use or excessive use. Any form of abuse is wrong. Any form of addiction is wrong even addiction to coffee or tea. If you are obsessed with anything or anyone you are in sin. Many Christian wives are obsessed with their husbands. Many Christians are consumed by their families; others are consumed by their ministries. They spend more time with the church than they spend with God. Once I heard of a pastor who went on a seven-day cruise but after the third day he started to repent for eating too much food and wasting time – time spent with his precious wife. The pastor wanted to be at the church working for the Lord.

Maybe he does not realize that he is obsessed with ministry. He is consumed with church work; he is addicted. What is lacking in the church is proper teaching. When we teach with the aim to bring freedom, people would make proper choices. When we preach from a point of fear, people become enslaved.

The second thing that is behind the teaching that drinking wine is a sin is control. The spirit of religion is a spirit of control and as I have said before it seeks to get the believer to adhere to rules rather than embrace a real relationship with Christ.

When a relationship with Christ is established, Holy Spirit controls the believer and guides him into all truth. The spirit of religion and legalism stands in the way of a person's real relationship with God. On matters that are controversial in the church, leadership power is used to institute laws and by-laws that people should adhere to. But buyers beware! When one's personal conviction is made a universal law over and against any other view, there is a serious problem. Let us look at the word of God to see how these types of matters should be handled.

Respect others conscience

Accept him whose faith is weak, without passing judgment on disputable matters.
Romans 14:1

Paul, the apostle, is dealing with what may have been a temporary and local problem in the Roman Church, but is also one continually confronting the Church and always demanding solution. In the Church at Rome there were apparently two lines of thought. There were some who believed that in

Christian liberty the old *taboos* were gone; they believed that the old food laws were now irrelevant. They also believed that Christianity did not consist in the special observance of any one day or days. *Paul makes it clear that this in fact is the position of real Christian faith.*

On the other hand, there were those who believed that it was wrong to eat meat; they believed in the rigid observance of the Sabbath. Paul calls this man *weak in the faith.* What does he mean by that? This person is weak in the faith for two reasons. (1) He has not yet discovered the meaning of Christian freedom; he is at heart still a legalist and sees Christianity as following a list of rules and regulations. (2) He has not yet liberated himself from a belief in the effectiveness of works. In his heart he believes that he can gain God's favor by doing certain things and abstaining from others. Basically he is still trying to earn a right relationship with God, and has not as yet accepted the way of grace. His emphasis is more of what he can do for God than of what God has done for him.

Paul encourages the stronger believers to welcome such a person and not to overwhelm him with criticisms. To this day in the Church, these two points of view are still present. There is the more liberal who sees no harm in many things and there is the narrower point of view, which is offended at many things in which the liberal person sees no harm.

Although Paul holds the broader view, he says that we must receive those with the narrower view as brotherly love. When we are confronted with such a person we must treat with him wisely. We must avoid irritating him. However much we may disagree, we must try to see the other person's point of view and to understand it. We must be careful to not take lightly what another person holds sacred and treat his belief with contempt. A man's conviction must be respected. We certainly will not be able to win anyone over to our position unless we have a genuine respect for his.

To deal with disputable matters in the church, Paul establishes a great principle. No man has any right to criticize another man's servant. The servant is answerable to his master alone. Now, all men are the servants of God. It is not open to us to criticize them, still less to condemn them. That right belongs to God alone. It is not in our judgment that a man stands or falls but in His. And, Paul goes on, if a man is honestly living out his principles as he sees them, God can make him able to stand.

Many a congregation and ministerial relationships are torn in two because those who hold broader views are angrily condescending of those whom they regard die-hard conservatives; and because those who are stricter in their outlook are hypercritical of those who, because of their freedom, do things they believe are wrong. *It is not open to us to condemn each other.* We must get rid of both contempt and censorship from the church. What if we are wrong? We must leave the judgment of others to God, and seek only to sympathize and to understand.

Different path to the same goal

One man considers one day more sacred than another; another man considers every day alike. Each one should be fully convinced in his own mind. 6 He who regards one day as special, does so to the Lord. He who eats meat, eats to the Lord, for he gives thanks to God; and he who abstains, does so to the Lord and gives thanks to God. 7 Romans 14:5-6

In the above verses, another disputable matter is addressed between the liberal and conservative. Those with the narrower view make a great deal of the observance of one special day. That was indeed a special characteristic of the Jews. More than once Paul was worried about people who made a fetish of observing days. He writes to the Galatians: "*You observe days, and months, and seasons, and years: I am afraid I have labored over you in vain*" (Galatians 4:10, 11).

He writes to the Colossians: "Let *no man pass judgment on you in questions of food and drink or with regard to a festival or a new moon or a Sabbath. These are only a shadow of what is to come; but the substance belongs to Christ*" (Colossians 2:16, 17). The Jews had made a dictatorship of the Sabbath, surrounding it with a jungle of regulations and prohibitions. It was not that Paul wished to wipe out any particular day. But behind the emphasis of keeping a day is the belief that Christianity consisted in observing one particular day. Paul had to wipe that out. It is not the day that we ought to worship, but the one who is the Lord of all days.

In spite of all that, Paul pleads for understanding between the both views. His point is that, however different both practices may be, their aim is the same. Both groups are serving God. That should be enough to unite us and *we should not allow differing practices to divide us.* But he insists on one thing. Whatever path a man chooses, let him be fully convinced in *his own mind.* His actions should be dictated not by *convention,* still less by *superstition,* but altogether by *conviction.* He should not do things simply because other people do them; he should not do them because he is governed by a system of semi-superstitious taboos; *he should do them because he has thought them out and reached the conviction that for him at least they are the right things to do.*

One of the curses of the church and the work of the spirit of legalism is when men think that their way of worship is the only way. No man should make his own practice the universal standard for all other people. We must do what we believe while remembering that someone thinks differently. We will do well to remember that in many matters. We have a duty to our convictions but we have an equal duty to allow others to have theirs without regarding them as sinners and outcasts.

Guided by the principle of love

Therefore let us stop passing judgment on one another. Instead, make up your mind not to put any stumbling block or obstacle in your brother's way. 14 As one who is in the Lord Jesus, I am fully convinced that no food b is unclean in itself. But if anyone regards something as unclean, then for him it is unclean. 15 If your brother is distressed because of what you eat, you are no longer acting in love. Do not by your eating destroy your brother for whom Christ died. 16 Do not allow what you consider good to be spoken of as evil. Romans 14:13-17

Throughout the history of the church up until today, many have failed right at this point – the point of love. Legalism blinds us and we cannot accept our brothers who may hold different views to ours. The kingdom on the other hand empowers us to deal with life and its differences. Let us look at some simple differences that we must accept daily. To a student of art, a certain picture might be a work of art, to someone else an obscene drawing. To one group of people a discussion might be an interesting, stimulating and mind-kindling experience, to someone else a succession of heresies, and even blasphemies.

Going to the movies, the opera, playing golf - a pleasure or pastime might seem to one quite permissible, and to another prohibited. A man may drink a glass of wine and it is harmless but that same glass of wine could ruin another. The thing itself is neither clean nor unclean; its character is determined by the person who sees it or does it.

That is what Paul is getting at here. There are certain things which a man strong in the faith may see no harm in doing; but, if a person who is weak in faith saw him doing them, his conscience would be shocked. Worst case scenario, if such a person were persuaded to do them, it would be disrespect and he would be outraged. For example, one man will genuinely see no harm in playing some outdoor game on Sunday, and he may be right; but another man's conscience is shocked at such a thing, and, if he were persuaded to take part in it, all the time he would have the haunting feeling that he was doing wrong.

Paul's advice is clear. *It is a Christian responsibility to think of everything, not as it affects us only, but also as it affects others.* Note that Paul is not saying that we must always allow our conduct to be dictated by the views of others; there are matters which are essentially matters of principle, and in them a person must make his own choice. But things that are neutral and indifferent; things are neither in themselves good or bad, it is Paul's conviction that in regard to such things we have no right to give offence to the more meticulous brother by doing them ourselves, or by persuading him to do them.

Life must be guided by the principle of love; and when it is, we will think, not so much of our right to do as we like as of our responsibilities to others. *We have no right to distress each other's conscience in the things which do not really matter.* Christian freedom must never be used as an excuse for rough riding over the genuine feelings of others. No pleasure is so important that it can justify bringing offence and grief, and even ruin, to others.

> *For the kingdom of God is not a matter of eating and drinking, but of righteousness, peace and joy in the Holy Spirit,* [18] *because anyone who serves Christ in this way is pleasing to God and approved by men.*
> [19] *Let us therefore make every effort to do what leads to peace and to mutual edification.* [20] *Do not destroy the work of God for the sake of food. All food is clean, but it is wrong for a man to eat anything that causes someone else to stumble.* Romans 14:17-20

Freedom and love go hand in hand

There is a kind of freedom that we have in Christ that most believers have not scratched the surface of. Just like the Jews whose lives were governed by so many rules and regulations, once they became followers of Christ and realized that there were no rituals to adhere to, some interpreted Christianity as a freedom to do what they liked. But we must remember that freedom and love must flow hand in hand. Yes, a person may be free to drink wine, eat meat or not eat meat, attend the movies, wear certain types of clothes, read certain books, listen to certain types of music, or any other thing but he must always consider the way of brotherly love.

Everything is permissible (allowable and lawful) for me; but not all things are helpful (good for me to do, expedient and profitable when considered with other things). Everything is lawful for me, but I will not become the slave of anything or be brought under its power. 1 Corinthians 6:12 AMP

In this particular scripture Paul is saying two things. He is saying that when it comes to eating and drinking he is totally free from the restrictions of the law – all things are lawful; all things are permissible. That is the freedom of the kingdom. With that freedom, Paul makes certain choices for his life. He thinks through his freedom and then exercises wisdom. And that is the way of the kingdom; people must be allowed to make choices for their own lives instead of being brought again back into bondage.

Paul reminds the Romans that Christianity does not consist in eating and drinking what one likes. Today, we too must remember that. No one is going to hell for eating or drinking anything. The kingdom consists in three great things, all of which are essentially *unselfish* things.

There is *righteousness*. This consists of living right before God. It also consists of living right before men. The moment we become a Christian, the feelings of the other person become *more* important than our own. Christianity means putting others first and self last. We cannot live righteously before men while doing what we like – we become slaves to ourselves.

There is *peace*. In the New Testament peace does not mean the absence of trouble; it is not a negative thing, but is intensely positive. It means everything that makes for a man's highest good. The Jews themselves often thought of peace as a state of right relationships between man and man. If we insist that Christian freedom means doing what we like, that is precisely the state we can never attain. Christianity consists of *personal relationships* with man and God. Therefore we should not use our freedom to destroy human relationship. *Right relationship is the hall mark of the kingdom.* It is only when we are able to develop and maintain right relationship with men that we will have peace.

There is *joy*. Christian joy can never be a selfish thing. It does not consist of making ourselves happy; it consists of making others happy. In our search for happiness we should not hurt and wound others. Joy in the kingdom is not individualistic; it is interdependent. Joy comes to us when we bring joy to others, even if it costs us our personal freedom. Christian freedom means that we are free to do what pleases Christ.

Respect the weaker brother

> *It is better not to eat meat or <u>drink wine</u> or to do anything else that will cause your brother to fall.*
> *22 So whatever you believe about these things keep between yourself and God. Blessed is the man who does not condemn*

himself by what he approves. 23 But the man who has doubts is condemned if he eats, because his eating is not from faith; and everything that does not come from faith is sin. Romans 14:21-23

Paul's advice is very practical and we should seek to pattern our decisions on disputable matters after it. First, Paul speaks to the one whom he labels strong in faith. This person knows that food and drink make no difference. He has grasped the principle of kingdom freedom. Well, then, let that freedom be something between him and God. He has reached this stage of faith; and God knows well that he has reached it. But that is no reason why he should flaunt his freedom in the face of the man who has not yet reached it.

A person who has reached a level of faith may come to the conclusion that his freedom in Christ gives him a perfect right to make a reasonable use of alcohol and, as far as he is concerned, it may be a perfectly safe decision, from which he runs no danger. But it may be that a younger person who admires him is watching him and looking up to him as an example. This younger person may be one of these people to whom alcohol is a dangerous even fatal thing. Should the free man use his freedom to go on setting an example which may well be the ruin of this young admirer? Or should he limit himself, not for his own sake, but for the sake of the one who follows in his footsteps?

The kingdom thing to do is to choose limitation over freedom for the sake of the other person. It is better to make this deliberate decision than to have the remorse of knowing that what was demanded as a pleasure has become death to someone else. Again and again, *in every sphere of life,* the believer is confronted with the fact that he must examine things, not only as they affect him, but also as they affect other people. We are all in one way or another "our brother's keeper." We are responsible not only for ourselves but for each other.

Secondly, Paul speaks to the one who is weak in faith. This person is still struggling with the legalistic way of Christianity. This person should not do anything because everyone else is doing it. If this person defies his conscience he is guilty of sin. If a man believes a thing to be wrong, then, **if *he does it*,** for *him* it is sin. A middle-of-the-road thing becomes a right thing only when it is done out of the real, reasoned conviction that it is right. In things that do not matter as in eating or drinking we all should be guided by our conscience.

Hypocrisy robs you of your conscience

When Judas, who had betrayed him, saw that Jesus was condemned, he was seized with remorse and returned the thirty silver coins to the chief priests and the elders. 4 "I have sinned," he said, "for I have betrayed innocent blood." "What is that to us?" they replied. "That's your responsibility."

5 So Judas threw the money into the temple and left. Then he went away and hanged himself.
6 The chief priests picked up the coins and said, "<u>It is against the law to put this into the treasury</u>, since it is blood money." 7 So they decided to use the money to buy the potter's field as a burial place for foreigners.
Matthew 27:3-7

The chief priest paid Judas thirty pieces of silver to betray Christ so that they could kill Him. The money came from the treasury. When Judas finally betrayed Jesus and could not live with himself anymore, he sought to give the money back to the priests and elders. They refused to take the money back into the treasury claiming it was blood money. Do you see the hypocrisy? It was okay to take money from the treasury to pay for Jesus' murder but it was unlawful to take it back. How convenient! That is hypocrisy.

Then the Jews led Jesus from Caiaphas to the palace of the Roman governor. By now it was early morning, and <u>to avoid ceremonial uncleanness the Jews did not enter the palace; they wanted to be able to eat the Passover.</u> 29 So Pilate came out to them and asked, "What charges are you bringing against this man?"
John 18:28-29

The Pharisees and high priests took Jesus to Pilate, the Roman Governor. Their goal was to have the governor convict and crucify Jesus. The religious order was on two tracks. One track was to kill Jesus and the other track was to be ceremonially clean so that they could eat the Passover. Do you see the hypocrisy? They refused to enter the Roman Palace because to do so would render them unclean and that would mean that they would not be able to eat Passover. So they stayed outside the building and shouted, "Crucify him." That way, after pleading with Pilate to kill Jesus, they could go home and be holy. Hypocrites!

Legalism focuses on outward appearances in its effort to appear holy but holiness is of the heart. A person does not look holy (although the Pharisees managed to pull that off). It is either he is holy or not. The legalistic person puts much emphasis on how he is viewed in the eyes of the public while in private he does the very thing he is against in public.

Hypocrisy focuses on self

> *One Sabbath, when Jesus went to eat in the house of a prominent Pharisee, he was being carefully watched. **2** There in front of him was a man suffering from dropsy. **3** Jesus asked the Pharisees and experts in the law, "Is it lawful to heal on the Sabbath or not?" **4** But they remained silent. So taking hold of the man, he healed him and sent him away.*

5 *Then he asked them, <u>"If one of you has</u> <u>a son a or an ox that falls into a well on the</u> <u>Sabbath day, will you not immediately pull</u> <u>him out?"</u>* **6** *And they had nothing to say.* Luke 14:1-6

In the above passage, Jesus challenges the religious and their hypocrisy. Jesus was at a Pharisees house and He knew they were watching Him. But there was a man who was suffering from dropsy whom Jesus wanted to heal. However, it was on the Sabbath day. Jesus challenged the system. Jesus asked if it was lawful to heal on the Sabbath. The experts of the law could not answer. Why? Deep down within the religious system and those who control it, they know what is right but they refuse to change. That is why it is hypocritical.

The religious system is set up by those whose only desire is to control, manipulate and take advantage of those within the system. **That is why you must buck the system.** The Pharisees made laws for the people that they knew were impossible to keep. Even they **would not keep** the law. *Then Jesus said to the crowds and to his disciples:* **2** *"The teachers of the law and the Pharisees sit in Moses' seat.* **3** *So you must obey them and do everything they tell you. But do not do what they do, for they do not practice what they preach.* **4** *They tie up heavy loads and put them on men's shoulders, but they themselves are not willing to lift a finger to move them.* Matthew 23:1-4 (See Acts 15: 10)

But as we look at the scriptures we see that there was a greater issue at hand. The Pharisees made laws that they **could not keep**; laws that were impossible for anyone to keep. *Now then, why do you try to test God by putting on the necks of the disciples <u>a yoke that neither we nor our fathers have been able to bear</u>?* Acts 15:10

The law became a yoke, a burden to the people. But much more than that, the religious order of the day tried to put that same yoke on Jesus. Jesus took it home; He got personal with them. If it was *your* son who needed to be healed, would it be such a big deal? What if it was *your* son or *your* ox that fell in a ditch at the beginning of Sabbath? Would you leave your son in the ditch overnight until Sabbath was over at the end of the following day? The experts of the law had no response. Jesus had once again successfully exposed the hypocrisy of the legalistic Pharisees.

Legalism is seen in a person who believes that going to the movies is a sin, but at home he would watch every possible show on television. That is hypocrisy! He watches the same movies that show at the movie theatre. Maybe he believes that he should not sit in the seat of the scornful. But if that is the case, I think he is living on the wrong planet.

What we are really dealing with is the spirit of exclusivism; the same spirit that characterized the Pharisees. The Pharisees refused to mix with anyone who was not a Pharisee and looked down on others who were not like them. It is a matter of straining out the gnat while eating a camel. It is called majoring on the minors.

If a person makes a law at least he should keep it. That is what Jesus was getting at with the Pharisees. They said that no healing should be done on the Sabbath. They made the law; God did not. It was their interpretation. Therefore, if the Pharisees were going to be so hard on others, when one of their family members needed help on the Sabbath, then he should suffer through the Sabbath just like everyone else.

That is why legalism must be confronted. It is a dangerous spirit. This spirit is present in our churches today. One church leader's daughter got pregnant. She is not married. His position is that he wants nothing to do with her or *his* grandchild and of course she was banned from the home. Of course, he is hurt, very disappointed and probably embarrassed as a pastor but what about the demonstration of mercy and faithful love. However, the spirit of legalism is so meticulous about the law that it blinds people from seeing human needs and flaws.

I heard a true story of a preacher who would not let his children watch television but would beat his wife; sometimes right before he goes to church. Do you see the hypocrisy? He shows his wife no mercy but is very concerned about a movie. The religious care more about rules and traditions than people. The kingdom of heaven is about God and His people. God is a people person.

There are so many forms of hypocrisy in the church today and we must recognize and confront it. It is like the evangelist who preaches against sin but manages to have an adulterous affair in every city he goes to preach. He is unfaithful to his wife and family but he has faith in God. The religious spirit is very selective in his obedience preferring to obey words that pertain to external changes while rejecting messages that address the inner man that, if received, would bring about change of character. The religious is more concerned about physical cleaning than spiritual cleaning. They would strain out a gnat but then eat a camel.

Chapter Five

The fifth woe – greed and self-indulgence

ๆ ๙

"Woe to you, teachers of the law and Pharisees, you hypocrites! You clean the outside of the cup and dish, but inside they are full of greed and self-indulgence. 26 Blind Pharisee! First clean the inside of the cup and dish, and then the outside also will be clean. Matthew 23:25-26

Greed and self-indulgence

The religious order would not admit that greed and self-indulgence are at the core of their activities, but Jesus was able to see right through them and was not afraid to confront their lifestyle. We know that the Pharisees were very meticulous about cleanliness but as far as Jesus was concerned, being clean on the outside begins with being clean on the inside. The spirit of religion is a master deceiver.

Much emphasis is placed on externalism, giving the false assumption that the whole is clean.

Naturally, the Pharisees would not touch anything that is unclean. The idea of uncleanness was a part of the Jewish Law. But the Pharisees were ultra clean. For a Jew this uncleanness was not physical uncleanness. An unclean vessel was not in our sense of the term, a dirty vessel. For a person to be ceremonially unclean meant that he could not enter the Temple or the synagogue; he was disqualified from the worship of God.

A man was unclean if, for instance, he touched a dead body, or came into contact with a Gentile. A woman was unclean if she had a hemorrhage, even if that hemorrhage was perfectly normal and healthy. If a person who was himself unclean touched any vessel, that vessel became unclean; and, thereafter, any other person who touched or handled the vessel became in turn unclean. It was, therefore, of paramount importance to have vessels cleansed; and the law for cleansing them was very complicated. These regulations seem unbelievable, but the Pharisees meticulously kept them.

Did Jesus have a problem with cleanliness? No! He had a problem with hypocrisy. As far as the Pharisees were concerned, the food or drink inside a vessel might have been obtained by cheating or extortion or theft; it might be lavish and gluttonous; that did not matter, *so long as the vessel itself was ceremonially clean.* This was another example of sweating the small stuff and letting the weightier matters go.

The religious order does not concern itself too much with how a man earns his money as long as he pays the tithe. A person does not have to be saved or attend church but the religious order would gladly receive their offering. They are more concerned about the outside of the cup and neglect the inside. Isn't a person's soul salvation more important than his money?

The cup of life

A deeper look at this fifth woe would reveal that the cup is symbolic of one's life. The religious emphasis is always external while the inside is neglected. Today, special robes and gowns are emphasized even in churches that claim spiritual freedom. Is it wrong to wear a robe? No! A person is free to wear whatever he chooses. However, clothing is not a standard for right living. Our righteousness does not come from what we wear but from Christ alone.

Externalism is dangerous because too much focus on the outside can lead to neglecting the inside. What we wear and how we appear are important but not at the expense of whom we really are. Today, people are more focused on their appearance than their character. This was the problem that Jesus had with the Pharisees. They placed so much emphasis on their special robes while at the same time paying little to no attention to what was in their hearts. As long as they appeared right they felt they had fulfilled their religious obligations.

Matthew 15:1-4 is a classic example of this, to which Jesus responded with a final word on the matter that resounded in the hearts of His listeners and should do the same with us today. Then some Pharisees and teachers of the law came to Jesus from Jerusalem and asked, "Why do your disciples break the tradition of the elders? They don't wash their hands before they eat!" Jesus replied, "And why do you break the command of God for the sake of your tradition?" It is clear that religion places more emphasis on tradition than the Word of God.

As far as Jesus was concerned, the washing of one's hands had little to do with spiritual matters. Washing of hands is a matter of proper hygiene. The religious have the ability to make natural laws appear spiritual. Once again the focus is on the outside. A person could be a crook but so long as he washes his hands or prays before meals, the religious would attach some form of righteousness to him.

Jesus always looked at the big picture – what really mattered was what was inside the cup. In Matthew 15:10-11, Jesus called the crowd to him and said, "Listen and understand. What goes into a man's mouth does not make him 'unclean,' but what comes out of his mouth that is what makes him 'unclean.'" Jesus continues in Matthew 15:17-20, "Don't you see that whatever enters the mouth goes into the stomach and then out of the body? But the things that come out of the mouth come from the heart, and these make a man 'unclean.' For out of the heart come evil thoughts, murder, adultery, sexual immorality, theft, false testimony, slander. These are what make a man 'unclean'; but eating with unwashed hands does not make him 'unclean.'"

The religious focuses on externalism – things that have little to no consequence in the kingdom while neglecting the matters that arise out of the heart. The condition of the inner man is more important than the condition of food or drink or clothes or car. Jesus charged the Pharisees with two things in this woe: extortion and self-indulgence (excess).

Woe to you, scribes and Pharisees, pretenders (hypocrites)! For you clean the outside of the cup and of the plate, but within they are full of extortion (prey, spoil, plunder) and grasping self-indulgence. Matthew 23:25 AMP

The religious turn worship into a business

Jesus charged the Pharisees with extortion and excess. Extortion is a strong word. Extortion is the act of plundering, robbery, and stealing. It is a predetermined plan to steal from someone. The Pharisees had the religious system set up so that they could rob the people. One example of this is found in Mark 11: 15-18.

On reaching Jerusalem, Jesus entered the temple area and began driving out those who were buying and selling there. He overturned the tables of the money changers and the benches of those selling doves, 16 and would not allow anyone to carry merchan-

dise through the temple courts. 17 And as he taught them, he said, "Is it not written: "'My house will be called a house of prayer for all nations' c? But you have made it 'a den of robbers.' d" 18 The chief priests and the teachers of the law heard this and began looking for a way to kill him, for they feared him, because the whole crowd was amazed at his teaching. Mark 11:15-18

In order to get the full impact of what Jesus did, it would help to have in our mind's eye a picture of the lay-out of the Temple precincts. There are two words used in the New Testament to describe temple. The first is *hieron*, which means *the sacred place*. This included the whole temple area. The temple area covered the top of Mount Zion and was about thirty acres in extent. It was surrounded by great walls which varied on each side, 1,000 to 1,300 feet in length.

There was a wide outer space called *the Court of the Gentiles*. Into it anyone, Jew or Gentile, might come. At the inner edge of the Court of the Gentiles was a low wall with tablets set into it which said that if a Gentile passed that point the penalty was death. The next court was called the *Court of the Women*. It was so called because unless women had come actually to offer sacrifice they might not proceed farther. Next was the *Court of the Israelites*. In it the congregation gathered on great occasions, and from it the offerings were handed by the worshippers to the priests. The inmost court was *the Court of the Priests.*

The other important word is *naos*, which means *the Temple proper*, and it was in the Court of the Priests that the Temple stood. The whole area, including all the different Courts, was the sacred precincts (*hieron*). The special building within the Court of the Priests was the Temple (*naos*).

It was the temple area that had become entirely secularized. It was meant to be a place of prayer and preparation, but in the time of Jesus, the priests – the religious had commercialized the temple with an atmosphere of buying and selling which made prayer and meditation impossible. What made it worse was that the business which went on in the Temple were sheer exploitation of the pilgrims. Who was in charge of the Temple? The Pharisees and Priests! The system was set-up to rob the worshippers. The religious order cannot be trusted; their motives are corrupt. Let us take a further look at how the system worked.

Every Jew had to pay a temple tax of one half shekel a year. That was a sum of 6p. It does not seem much but it has to be evaluated against the fact that the standard day's wage for a working man was 3½p. That tax had to be paid in one particular kind of coinage. For ordinary purposes Greek, Roman, Syrian, Egyptian, Phoenician, Tyrian coinages were all equally valid. But this tax had to be paid in shekels of the sanctuary. It was paid at the Passover time.

Jews came from all over the world to Passover and with all kinds of currencies. When they went to have their money changed they had to pay a fee of 1p and should their coin exceed the tax, they had to pay another 1p before they got their change. *This was extortion.* Most pilgrims had to pay this extra 2p before they could pay their tax. We must remember that that was half a day's wage, which for most men was a great deal of money.

As for the sellers of doves—doves were a choice bird in the sacrificial system (Leviticus 12:8, 14:22, 15:14). A sacrificial victim had to be without blemish. *Doves could be bought cheaply enough outside, but the temple inspectors would be sure to find something wrong with them*, and worshippers were advised to buy them at the temple stalls instead. No matter how careful the worshipper was, his offering could never be good enough to be accepted by the priests. The only acceptable offerings were the ones sold by the priests themselves. What a scam!

Doesn't this have a familiar ring to it? I once heard of a pastor who had miracle anointing oil from Israel for sale. The price was a whooping $1,000 per bottle. But that was not all. An appointment had to be made so that he could be consulted on how to use the oil. *The consultation fee was another $200.00.* This is a sure sign of a merchandiser; one of the trade marks of the religious spirit.

The religious uses ministry as a platform to sell all kinds of products with the sole intent of making money. They will use gimmicks, tricks and any scheme to promote and manipulate people into purchasing their products. One pastor "under the anointing," cut up pieces of a plant from the church and sold it at

$500.00 a piece. The people were so deceived – they bought it. Merchandisers are not short on gimmicks. Their goal is to get at the believers money through manipulation and deception. Watch out for miracle oils, soaps that can wash away witchcraft, prophetic healing juices, and the pastor's towel cut up in pieces to be used as prayer cloths, miracle manna, and many other gimmicks.

Do not be deceived. Not every building with a church sign on the front is a church that Jesus is building. Some people have entered the ministry for the sole purpose of making money. For them it is a business opportunity. While there are many who have embarked on the call to ministry by the Spirit of God, some of them have been enticed and drawn away by the power of money and the things it can buy.

The religious does not only have products designed to scam you of your money, they offer prophesies and prayer with the same objective. At a meeting, one prophet called out a woman who was sick with cancer and told her that the Lord was going to heal her. The woman got so excited; she was desperate. The prophet then offered her an envelope, told her that she must pay $365.87 in order to get her healing. What a let down! God is a healing God but He does not do it for money.

Then there are others who would sell prophecies. The goal is to fleece the weak and vulnerable in the body of Christ. These are the saints who are the most gullible to these crooks behind the "cloth". Once I went to a conference where everything was centered on the "man of God." There was a very huge picture of him on the pulpit. He came out and spoke for about 45 minutes. Then it was time for the punch line. If a person wanted the "prophet" to prophesy to him, he had to get $200.*00 in silver* to bring to the "man of God." There was a table provided to make the exchange. For $100.00, a person can get a prophetic word from one of the "prophet's" disciples. *I left!*

Have you ever received a letter in the mail, encouraging you to send in your prayer request with a special offering of $79.98 or some other ridiculous figure? It is an attempt to rob you. If you send it in, know that you are being fleeced. Some merchandisers are so desperately smart that they would not attach any special amount. They will leave that up to you. Do not send it in.

Millions of those letters are sent out with the hope that at least a few hundred thousand people would respond. You do the math. If you have extra money to give away, take it to your local church and either give a special offering or be a blessing to your spiritual father. It is he who has the responsibility to watch for your soul.

If your leader is a merchandiser, then you need to make plans to leave. He would pray for God to bless you so that he can be blessed. His motive will corrupt every act of service he performs. He would preach you happy so that he could take a big offering at the end of the service. If a person's motivation for ministry is money, he is not a servant of God.

How can you judge someone's motives? You can know them by their fruit. Examine the fruit! Look for set patterns in ministry. If every time a person preaches the word, God tells him to take a $5,000.00 offering, that is a pattern of impure motive. If a person has a deliverance ministry and is always marketing something from soap to saw dust to miracle water that is a pattern of merchandising. Buyer, beware!

Merchandisers are people who use the Body of Christ for the sole purpose of making money. There is way too much buying and selling of almost everything in the church today and it is an indication of the level of religiosity that has overtaken the church.

Please do not misunderstand me. I am all for the proper distribution of ministry resources, including books, CDs and DVDs. We need these materials in the church to help us study the word and keep us up to date with what God *is* saying to the church. Some of the best books I've read are not available in most Christian book stores; I got them at conferences or on-line. However, materials must be offered in an appropriate fashion without manipulation and coercion.

The Pharisees and priests, made a business out of worship. They preyed on the vulnerability of the people and it caused Jesus to fume with anger – righteous indignation. When pilgrims traveled to Jerusalem for the Passover, they had to present an offering to the priest. But it was the same priests, in conjunction with the teachers of the law – the Pharisees that were in control of the "offering business." Outside doves cost as little as 31/2p a pair; inside they cost as much as 75p. Do you see the vast difference in the prices? No matter how hard a person tried, his turtle dove could never meet the standard set by the high priest. Why? The High Priest would deny the turtle dove so that the pilgrim would patronize his business.

Under the religious system, the poor and vulnerable got swindled. The temple court had become a type of Jericho road. The road from Jerusalem to Jericho was notorious for its robbers. It was a narrow winding road, passing between rocky ruins. Amidst the rocks were caves where the bandits lay in wait. Apparently, the pilgrims had more to fear from the bandits in the temple than those in the caves of "the Jericho road."

The religious are those who have moved away from the essence of true worship and into a form of godliness. They resort to the exploitation of the worshippers. The Temple authorities were treating the pilgrims not as worshippers, not even as human beings, *but as things to be exploited for their own ends*. Every person represented a dollar sign. Man's exploitation of man always provokes the wrath of God, and doubly so when it is made under the cloak of religion.

Commercialization and merchandising bring desecration of God's holy place. The religious have lost their sense of the presence of God in the house of God. This is a serious violation; one which Jesus did not condone. We too must rise up with a loud no in our mouths to this type of manipulation in the church. The church is not for sale. Everyday, your declaration should be: I would not be manipulated, bullied or bought.

Not only were the Pharisees extortionists; they were self-indulgent. They were full of excess. God is a God of abundance but he is not a God of excess. *Excess means a going beyond what is regarded as customary or proper; immoderate indulgence; intemperance in eating, drinking, etc.* God gives with a purpose. When we enter the realm of excess, we move outside of the realm of purpose. That is when a person has twelve cars just sitting in the garage; he does not even drive them. It is when there is so much food in the house that you throw out more than you consume.

Jesus got mad because it is not right to be an extortionist and self-indulgent at the same time. If a person has too much already, why does he need to rob others? That is wickedness! Jesus said the Pharisees – the religious were full of excess. They had lost the ability to control their lust for more. Greed had taken over their lives. Today, the religious spirit is alive in many people, especially leaders who rob the people of God so that they can lavish themselves with excess. And even in their excess they demand more. The religious spirit pretends to be a Christian but would rob you of your money – the person is really a crook, not a Christian. Jesus calls the religious hypocrites – play actors; they are not real.

Chapter Six

The sixth woe – false impression and disguise
❧ ❧

"Woe to you, teachers of the law and Pharisees, you hypocrites! You are like whitewashed tombs, which look beautiful on the outside but on the inside are full of dead men's bones and everything unclean. 28 In the same way, on the outside you appear to people as righteous but on the inside you are full of hypocrisy and wickedness. Matthew 23:27-28

The spirit of false impression

Again the religious spirit is a master at false impression. Everything looks clean on the outside to make believe that it is also clean on the inside. Jesus calls this hypocrisy and exposes the true motives of the religious order. With the religious, nothing is ever what it appears to be – there is always an ulterior rotten motive.

To call a Jew especially a Pharisee a tomb was a terrible insult. The Pharisees prided themselves as the "clean ones." When Jesus called the Pharisees whitewashed tombs, they understood exactly what He meant. One of the most common places for tombs was by the wayside and anyone who touched a dead body became unclean (Numbers 19:16). Therefore, anyone who came into contact with a tomb automatically became unclean.

At the time of the Passover Feast the roads of Palestine were crowded with pilgrims. For a man to become unclean on his way to the Passover Feast would be a disaster, because that meant he would be debarred from sharing in it. It was then Jewish practice in the month of Adar to whitewash all wayside tombs, so that no pilgrims might accidentally come into contact with one of them and be rendered unclean.

So, as a man traveled the roads of Palestine on a spring day, these tombs would glint white, and almost lovely, in the sunshine; but within they were full of bones and bodies whose touch would defile. That, said Jesus, was a precise picture of what the Pharisees were. Their outward actions were the actions of intensely religious men; their inward hearts were foul and full of things that defile and decompose with sin.

He went on: "What comes out of a man is what makes him 'unclean.' 21 For from within, out of men's hearts, come evil thoughts, sexual immorality, theft, murder, adultery, 22 greed, malice, deceit, lewdness, envy, slander, arro-gance and folly. **23** *All these evils come from inside and make a man 'unclean.'"* Mark 7:20-23

This statement must have run like a dagger through the hearts of the Pharisees. They were so locked into the law that they could not see the true essence of cleanliness. They were blind. Jesus makes it clear that a person is not defiled by what he eats or drinks. A person is not defiled because he eats pork or drinks wine. The true focus of being clean must be on the heart because that is the source of all evil.

Jesus' problem with the Pharisees was that they were so meticulous about outward cleanliness but paid little to no attention to the condition of the heart. In other words, the Pharisees were like the very tombs that they did not want to touch – looked white and beautiful on the outside but dark and decaying on the inside.

It does not matter how a cemetery may be dressed up, it remains a dead house – a place for the dead. The religious have been running around the church without anyone pressing for more than just what looks good. The religious church places a strong emphasis on how the congregants dress especially females.

In some churches women are not allowed to wear sleeveless shirts and skirts must be very loose and long. So long as something looks holy on the outside, the church accepts it. But it is time for the church to rise up and demand authenticity. We must move beyond the superficial and get to the reality of true Christ centeredness. We must place more importance on the inner condition of the heart and refrain from being impressionists.

The spirit of disguise

The religious are dead on the inside because they never submit to God's authority. A person can start attending church but never surrender to change. As a result, he can place a strong emphasis on outward appearance, adapt church lingo and disguise himself as a Christian. Externally, life looks Christian. Outwardly, he appears righteous but inwardly is full of hypocrisy, iniquity, and death. Some time ago I went to a function with some of the members of our local church. When I was introduced as their pastor, people were visibly shocked. Their response was that I did not look like a pastor. My question was, "What does a pastor look like?"

The religious place high emphasis clothing. They can be seen with robes, collars, and crosses around their necks. In many religious circles this is manda-tory attire. A person can be reprimanded for noncom-pliance to "protocol." However, the same passion is not demonstrated on matters of holiness and purity of heart.

For instance, in one religious organization where religious attire is mandatory for its leaders, some priests were found guilty of raping and other forms of sexual abuse of congregants. Jesus calls this hypocrisy and rightly so. The priests looked holy on the outside but on the inside were death and decay – sinister minds. How could a piece of cloth be more important to God than a person's heart? For the record, God cares much more about the inner condition of a person's heart than what he wears or how he appears.

Remember when Samuel went to Jesse's house to anoint a new king to rule over Israel? (1 Samuel 16) When they arrived, Samuel saw Eliab and thought, "Surely the LORD's anointed stands here before the LORD." But the LORD said to Samuel, "Do not consider his appearance or his height, for I have rejected him. The LORD does not look at the things man looks at. Man looks at the outward appearance but the LORD looks at the heart." 1 Samuel 16:6-7

Samuel would have chosen Eliab and anointed him as king. He would have been wrong. Appearances can be misleading. If we judge others only on how they appear we can be wrong. Looks are deceiving! We must get beyond the surface of things and people and see them for whom they really are. God is concerned about character, something that leaves much to be desired in many in our churches today, especially those in leadership.

The religious are also seen in churches that demand congregants dress a certain way, even wear certain colors on certain days. For example, on first Sundays or Pentecost Sunday, congregants are required to wear white. No only are congregant expected to dress according to the dress code of the church but those who cannot afford to conform will either not show up or feel uncomfortable. In the religious church people are not free to wear what they feel comfortable with.

The Bible is clear that women should dress moderately (1Timothy 2: 9-10). This is also true for men. The religious decide for others what is moderate and what is not. They make rules and regulations to ensure congregants, especially women dress "right." The religious spirit seeks to control people by using the word of God out of its proper context.

The religious church places more emphasis on the sanctuary, the sound system, and the floral arrangements than on the spiritual growth and development of the saints. As long as congregants show up for Sunday morning services with their tithes and offerings, these churches are happy to continue with business as usual.

The religious are people who boast about past moves of God but reject present day moves of God. This is the saddest part of it all. Most of these religious ministries started as vibrant, radical churches. They find their genesis in revival. What happened? The spirit of religion got a strangle hold on these churches and would not let go. All the religious is left with is a history of the past while the present is void of life. In my book *"The New Order Leader,"* I warn about this spirit that lurks and waits for new vibrant ministries to become complacent or proud and then it makes its move, striking the church like a python and slowly squeezes the vibrancy, passion, and life out of the church. What is left is a shell of the church where the spirit of religion rules.

The spirit of wickedness

Jesus levels another serious charge against the Pharisees – wickedness. Wickedness is the state of being wicked; a mental disregard for justice, righteousness, truth, honor, virtue; evil in thought and life; depravity; sinfulness; criminality. Wickedness is sin taken to another level. It begins with a thought, then a deed, then a character, and finally a destiny. In life, men increase in wickedness till they lose all desire for that which is good in the sight of God and men. The Pharisees were a classic example of this. They degenerated into men that called evil good, and good evil; that put darkness for light, and light for darkness" (<u>Isaiah 5:20</u>).

This spirit of wickedness is still prevalent in today's church. Some religious leaders would put curses on members who leave the church. Because the motivation of the religious for ministry is wrong, they never want anyone to leave the church. It is a threat to their kingdom. Even if there are mature saints in the church, the religious would not release them into ministry – it is a one-man-show. God usually would allow some form of confusion to break out, so that those who should be sent out leave. The religious spirit will begin to move in wickedness and witchcraft. Watch out for this spirit.

Chapter Seven

The seventh woe – Killing the prophets
ৎৎ ৎৎ

"Woe to you, teachers of the law and Pharisees, you hypocrites! You build tombs for the prophets and decorate the graves of the righteous. 30 And you say, 'If we had lived in the days of our forefathers, we would not have taken part with them in shedding the blood of the prophets.' 31 So you testify against yourselves that you are the descendants of those who murdered the prophets.
Matthew 23:29-31

A murderous spirit

Jesus charged the religious Pharisees with being descendants of murderers. Murder was in their genes. They, just like their parents, were murderers. The Scribes and Pharisees kept the tombs of the martyrs and beautified their memorials, claiming that, if they had lived in the old days they would not have slain the prophets and the men of God. But that is precisely what they would have done - and precisely what they were going to do.

Jesus' charge is that the history of Israel is the history of the murder of the men of God by the religious order. Jesus claimed that Abel was killed by a religious spirit. The story of Cain and Abel is told in Genesis 4. As we look at it we will learn more about the spirit of religion and how dangerous it is.

Now Abel kept flocks, and Cain worked the soil. In the course of time Cain brought some of the fruits of the soil as an offering to the LORD. But Abel brought fat portions from some of the firstborn of his flock. The LORD looked with favor on Abel and his offering, but on Cain and his offering he did not look with favor. So Cain was very angry, and his face was downcast. Genesis 4:2-5

The religious is always competing and comparing

Both Cain and Abel offered sacrifices to God. Abel's was accepted and Cain's was not. What was Cain's response? Anger! He could not be happy for his brother. He could not deal with his own loss. It is clear that Cain viewed worship as a competition. In the kingdom there is no competition; there is completion. God did not judge Cain because of what he brought; He refused to accept his offering because of the content of his heart. His heart was not right before the Lord.

Then the LORD said to Cain, "Why are you angry? Why is your face downcast? 7 If you do what is right, will you not be accepted? But if you do not do what is right, sin is crouching at your door; it desires to have you, but you must master it." (Genesis 4:6-7) Cain became angry because he lost. God was clear; sin was at the door of Cain's heart. God rejected his offering so that he could deal with his sin but instead of mastering it he succumbed to it.

This is a classic picture of the religious order. Once again, as long as everything looks picture perfect on the outside the religious is happy. They refuse to deal with matters of the heart. In fact, if you want to be on the hit-list of any religious institution or people just begin to point out the errors of their beliefs and you can consider it a done deal – you are on the list. Get ready for death threats and character assassination. The religious spirit is a murderous spirit. God warned Cain of his sin but he refused to listen to God. This is characteristic of the religious spirit.

Today, the religious ministry is always in competition with the neighboring churches. If one ministry starts to grow then the religious church, instead of celebrating what God is doing, will set out to kill the move of God. Why? Jealousy! If one ministry is on television, the religious leader wants to be on television too. I recently had to ask a pastor to examine his motives for going on television. If we do ministry just because everyone else is doing it without any clear mandate from the Lord, we will be operating out of a spirit of religion.

God gives to each person and to each ministry as He wills. To one He gave five talents, to another two and to the other one (Matthew 25). This should teach us to never compare ourselves and ministry with others. John was wise in his response to his disciples when they brought news of losing members to Jesus' ministry. To this John replied, "A man can receive only what is given him from heaven (John 3:27-28). There was no competition between John and Jesus' ministry. It is the reason why John was able to decrease so that Jesus could increase. His heart was right towards Jesus. Both ministries complemented and completed each other.

Religious people will be there for you as long as you are struggling. Why? It makes them feel important. They will always refer to the time when you were struggling and how they came along right in the nick of time. Once God begins to bless and increase you and the favor of God is evident on your life, religious people will open up your past. Their goal is to keep you in their claws, never releasing you to fulfill your destiny. They will kill you. Abel never lived to fulfill his purpose. Religious people cannot be trusted. They will be with you as long as you agree with them and serve their purpose but the moment you start to get ahead they will come against you.

The religious resist change

Every prophet after Abel was killed by a religious spirit. Jesus says that the righteous men from Abel to Zacharias were murdered by the religious spirit.

The murder of Zacharias is told in 2 Chronicles 24:20–22.

> *Then the Spirit of God came upon Zechariah son of Jehoiada the priest. He stood before the people and said, "This is what God says: 'Why do you disobey the LORD's commands? You will not prosper. Because you have forsaken the LORD, he has forsaken you.'"* **21** *But they plotted against him, and by order of the king they stoned him to death in the courtyard of the LORD's temple.* **22** *King Joash did not remember the kindness Zechariah's father Jehoiada had shown him but killed his son, who said as he lay dying, "May the LORD see this and call you to account."* 2 Chronicles 24:20-22

Zechariah lost his life because he spoke the truth to Israel. Joash, the king, gave approval for the people to stone him to death in the Temple court. The leader of God's people is behind the killing. Instead of agreeing with the priest and returning to Yahweh, the religious kills the prophet so that they could continue to worship Asherah poles and idols (2 Chronicles 24: 18).

The religious does not want to change. They have been doing church for a long time and they do not want to change. The only way to access the kingdom reality is through constant change, adjustments, and transitions. That is why John came preaching repentance and lost his life. Jesus preached repentance and gave his life. The religious would rather kill the prophet before they change.

True prophetic ministry and religion cannot co-exist. I have seen prophetic ministries lose their edge because of the spirit of religion. It is like a python that slowly squeezes the life out of the church until it becomes cold and lifeless. Prophets are designated to proclaim and protect the purposes of God on the earth. Surely, the Sovereign LORD does nothing without revealing his plan to his servants, the prophets (Amos 3:7). Whenever Israel abandoned Yahweh to worship other gods and idols, God sent prophets to declare His mind and to call them back to Yahweh. Instead of changing, the religious leaders would rather kill the prophets of God.

The religious has lost all sense of holiness. Of course, they have their own form of godliness – special robes, clothes, jewelry (rings and crosses), special lingo etc. Holiness means to be loyal to Yahweh *only*. How could the leadership of Israel be loyal to Yahweh and worship idols? How could a religious leader be loyal to Yahweh and blatantly disobey His word? How could he kill the prophets of Yahweh who bring His message? How could the religious today claim loyalty to Yahweh and refuse to embrace present moves of God?

From beginning to end, the history of Israel is the rejection, and often the slaughter, of the prophet of God. Here indeed is the tragedy; the nation which God chose and loved had turned their hands against Him, and the day of reckoning was to come. Jesus is quite clear that the murder taint is still there. He knows that now He must die, and that in the days to come His messengers will be persecuted, ill-treated, rejected and slain. The same religious spirit that killed the prophets of the past was now honoring them while plotting to kill Jesus and future prophets. The cycle continues.

The religious makes monuments of the tombs of the martyred prophets killed by the previous religious generation while they kill present day prophets. For example, Saul was a Pharisee; he presided over the stoning to death of Stephen. When they heard this, they were furious and gnashed their teeth at him. But Stephen, full of the Holy Spirit, looked up to heaven and saw the glory of God, and Jesus standing at the right hand of God. "Look," he said, "I see heaven open and the Son of Man standing at the right hand of God." At this they covered their ears and, yelling at the top of their voices; *they all rushed at him, dragged him out of the city and began to stone him.* Meanwhile, the witnesses laid their clothes at the feet of a young man named *Saul.* Acts 7:54-58

Viper ministry

The ministry of the religious order is like that of a viper. Vipers are snakes characterized by the presence of poisonous fangs fused to the moveable maxilla (upper jaw). Their venom is strongly hemolytic, which acts to destroy blood corpuscles and vessels. Thus they pose a real danger to human beings.

It is the mouth of the religious that has the power to kill. They can open their mouths and spew out enough poison to kill the messenger and the message of God. Every time they open their mouth you can expect some poison to be released. The religious would often release poison against other ministries so that members of their congregation would not visit or support them.

The religious would release poison against present moves of God so as to keep control over God's people. The religious knows wherever the spirit of the Lord is there is freedom. In order to keep people in bondage, the religious will release poison into anything birthed by Holy Spirit. The religious will say things like, "The apostolic and prophetic is not for today." The religious will seek to poison ministries that bring healing and deliverance from demons to God's people. They would say that speaking in tongues is not for today.

The religious ministry is a kill-joy ministry. They do not want you to experience the full freedom of what Christ has secured for you. They want you to serve God not as a son but as a slave to their traditions. Sons of God are free. If the religious see you operating in freedom, they will say that you are not saved and seek to bring you back into bondage. It is a viper ministry.

Most vipers give birth to fully developed offspring, while only a few species lay eggs (oviparous). This is powerful. The offspring of the religious hit the ground running – fully-developed religious sons. It is a birds-of-a-feather flock together syndrome. Vipers are poisonous snakes. The religious are people to be avoided if you want to stay alive. Jesus calls them a brood of viper – where there is one, there is more. They seldom travel alone.

But when he saw many of the Pharisees and Sadducees coming to where he was baptizing, he said to them: "You brood of vipers! Who warned you to flee from the coming wrath? 8 Produce fruit in keeping with repentance. 9 And do not think you can say to yourselves, 'We have Abraham as our father.' I tell you that out of these stones God can raise up children for Abraham. 10 The ax is already at the root of the trees, and every tree that does not produce good fruit will be cut down and thrown into the fire. Matthew 3:7-10

In the days of John the Baptist, many of the Pharisees and Sadducees came to his baptism but he would not touch them. They wanted to align themselves with John but they did not want to change. Today, in many churches, people have jumped on the Christian bandwagon but refuse to change. Hence the reason for so many religious churches today.

John told the religious that the only way to escape the coming wrath was through repentance – change. The religious want to join the church but retain control over his life. He still wants to live his life according to the world's standard while he attends church every Sunday morning. The ax is laid at the root of the tree that does not produce fruit or evidence of change – it will be cut down.

What the Pharisees were doing was characteristic of vipers. When vipers see the harvesters coming or when fire approaches, they would flee. The religious does not truly repent, they just flee from the coming wrath. They do not want to burn. In the church you can recognize the religious – they are there to escape hell; they do not want to burn. They seldom live out the purposes of God; they just want to make it into heaven. They come to church just to stay saved. No wonder Jesus called the religious hypocrites.

Chapter Eight

Steps to Freedom
ও ও

Religion and the kingdom cannot co-exist. The church must be free from the evil workings of this spirit so that it can fulfill the true purpose of God. We must see this spirit as evil and refuse to accept and abide with it. If you have been under the power of this spirit, you must take the steps necessary to be free. Here are some things you can do. Remember, to break free is only the first part; you must maintain your freedom.

Repentance

In order to break free from religion, repentance is absolutely necessary. Most people have only a partial understanding of the word and that is why real change is seldom accomplished. Both John and Jesus were clear on repentance and only those who did repent were able to access the kingdom of heaven. Remember, the goal of religion is to stop you, and ultimately the church, from embracing the kingdom of heaven on earth. Repentance is the only way through which a person can enter the kingdom of heaven.

> *In those days John the Baptist came, preaching in the Desert of Judea* [2] *and saying, "Repent, for the kingdom of heaven is near."* [3] *This is he who was spoken of through the prophet Isaiah: "A voice of one calling in the desert, 'Prepare the way for the Lord, make straight paths for him.'"* Matthew 3:1-3

> *From that time on Jesus began to preach, "Repent, for the kingdom of heaven is near."* Matthew 4:17

In order to get an accurate idea of the precise New Testament meaning of this highly important word it is necessary to consider its approximate synonyms in the original Hebrew and Greek.

The Hebrew word *naham*, implies difficulty in breathing, hence, "to pant," "to sigh," "to groan." Repent - *"to Pant,"* or *"to Sigh"* came to signify "to lament" or "to grieve." When the emotion was produced by the desire of good for others, it merged into compassion and sympathy, and when incited by a consideration of one's own character and deeds it means "to rue," "to repent." This word is translated "repent" about 40 times in the Old Testament, and in nearly all cases it refers to God.

The LORD was grieved that he had made man on the earth, and his heart was filled with pain. Genesis 6:6

When God saw what they did and how they turned from their evil ways, he had compassion and did not bring upon them the destruction he had threatened. Jonah 3:10

For example, in Genesis 6 and Jonah 3: 10, God is represented as repenting when He delayed punishment or when threatened evils have been averted by genuine reformation. The principal idea is not personal relation to sin, either in its experience of grief or in turning from an evil course. Yet the results of sin are manifest in its use. God's heart is grieved at man's iniquity, and in love He bestows His grace, or in justice He terminates His mercy. *It indicates the aroused emotions of God which prompt Him to a different course of dealing with the people.*

Repent also means "*to turn*" or "*to return*." The term *shubh*, is most generally employed to express the Scriptural idea of genuine repentance. It is used extensively by the prophets, and conveys the idea of a radical change in one's attitude toward sin and God. *It implies a conscious, moral separation, and a personal decision to forsake sin and to enter into fellowship with God.* It is employed to indicate the thorough spiritual change which God alone can effect.

In the New Testament, the term *metamelomai* literally signifies to have a feeling or care, concern or regret; it expresses the emotional aspect of repentance. To repent can mean "to be careful" or "to be concerned with." The feeling indicated by the word may indicate genuine repentance, or it may degenerate into mere remorse (Matthew 21:29, 32; 27:3). Judas repented only in the sense of regret, remorse, and not in the sense of the abandonment of sin.

To repent also means "to change the mind." The word *metanoeo*, expresses the true idea of the spiritual change implied in a sinner's return to God. The term signifies "to have another mind," to change the opinion or purpose with regard to sin. It is equivalent to the Old Testament word "turn" and is used by John the Baptist, Jesus, and the apostles (Matthew 3:2; Mark 1:15; Acts 2:38). Repentance produces fruit appropriate to the new life (Matthew 3:8).

The word *epistrepho*, another New Testament word used to bring out more clearly the distinct change wrought in repentance. It means "to turn upon," "to turn over," "to turn unto." It is used quite frequently in Acts to express the positive side of a change involved in repentance, or to indicate the return to God of which the turning from sin is the negative aspect. Repentance involves the turning away from sin and the turning towards God. The two concepts are inseparable and complementary. Repentance is used to express the spiritual transition from sin to God (Acts 9:35; 1 Thessalonians 1:9).

We must be very careful not to confuse repentance with penitence. Penitence signifies pain, grief, distress, rather than a change of mind. For centuries, the church has been corrupted by presenting grief over sin rather than the abandonment of sin as the main idea of repentance. The words of the ancient prophets, of Jesus, and of the apostles show that the change of mind is the dominant idea of the words used to mean repentance.

To break free from the spirit of religion, a person must:

o   Make a personal decision to forsake human traditions, vain philosophies, church rituals, legalistic views, and every form of godliness and surrender the control of his whole life to God through Jesus Christ.

o   Move beyond feelings of sadness and remorse about the state of the church or his life and develop a real care and concern for the true purposes of God and His church in the earth.

o   Fully embrace the principles and values of the kingdom of heaven and begin to practice them.

o   Pursue different ways of functioning in ministry.

o   Transition from the religious paradigm of ministry to the kingdom model of ministry.

o   Produce evidence of a new life.

Submission to the government of the local church

Obey your leaders and submit to their authority. They keep watch over you as men who must give an account. Obey them so that

*their work will be a joy, not a burden, for that
would be of no advantage to you.* Hebrews
13:17

It is absolutely necessary that you be a part of
the right kind of church. You must find a Spirit-led,
Bible-teaching church and get connected to it. Submit
to and obey the leadership of that local church and
begin to serve there. The spirit of religion is behind
people who move about from church to church, never
being planted and as a result never producing fruit.

Once you are in the right church, dig your heels
in and begin to serve the vision of the house. Make a
decision to be there for the long haul. Attend services
regularly and apply the word of God to your life daily.
Continue to make kingdom adjustments to your life
so that you do not become stale and outdated. Seek
to learn and grow.

Maintain your freedom

*It is for freedom that Christ has set us free.
Stand firm, then, and do not let yourselves
be burdened again by a yoke of slavery.*
Galatians 5:1

Paul dealt with the question of freedom with the
Galatian Church. They struggled with legalism. There
was a legalistic movement spreading its leaven and
the church was once again being seduced. Watch out
for teachings that promote salvation by works. Christ
has set you free; stay free. You are free to worship

and serve God. Watch out for restrictions in worship. The local church should be a place where the saints can express their worship. If there is no freedom in worship or if worship is being curtailed, you are probably in a religious church.

You are free to live a happy vibrant lifestyle. Watch out for rules that seek to take away your joy. Christ wants you to be happy and He died so that you can have abundant life. Watch out for the list that includes what you should and shouldn't eat or drink, where you should or shouldn't go, what you should or shouldn't wear. Life in Christ is about a relationship and not about rules. Be led by the spirit and do whatever is pleasing to Him.

Examine your motives

For the appeal we make does not spring from error or impure motives, nor are we trying to trick you. **4** *On the contrary, we speak as men approved by God to be entrusted with the gospel. We are not trying to please men but God, who tests our hearts.* **5** *You know we never used flattery, nor did we put on a mask to cover up greed — God is our witness.* **6** *We were not looking for praise from men, not from you or anyone else.* 1 Thessalonians 2:3-6

Motive is that which causes a person to act in a certain way or do a certain thing. It is the goal or object of a person's actions. The religious almost always operate with impure motives. The word used for *impurity* (*akatharsia*) often has to do with sexual impurity. It really has to do with gaining pleasure. If money, power, or pleasure (sexual or otherwise) is the goal of a person's preaching or service, then his motives are impure.

Whatever you do, do it to please the Lord. Watch out for greed. The body of Christ is in trouble today and greed is playing a critical role in it all. The spirit of consumerism and acquisitiveness has found its way into the hearts of God's people and the damage is collateral. With the spirit of greed on the loose, trickery has become the order of the day. Prophecies and prayers given to unsuspecting saints in order to get at their bank accounts or form unhealthy soulties are evidence of trickery. Service given with the hope of gaining anyone's approval or a promotion is evidence of an impure heart.

Paul was accused of seeking to please men rather than to please God. No doubt that rose from the fact that he preached the liberty of the gospel and the freedom of grace as against the slavery of legalism. There are always people who do not think that they are being holy unless they are being unhappy; and any one who preaches a gospel of joy will find great opposition. This is exactly what happened to Jesus.

Prestige can also corrupt a person's motive. This is especially true for those in the five-fold ministry. The need to be accepted is a constant danger that the preacher faces. If you are a five-fold minister, make sure it is your message that is displayed. Watch out for when you begin to take credit for how God is using you. Do whatever you must to maintain a pure heart. *How can a young man keep his way pure? By living according to your word.* Ps 119:9

Become a student of the Word

All Scripture is God-breathed and is useful for teaching, rebuking, correcting and training in righteousness, 17 so that the man of God may be thoroughly equipped for every good work. 2 Timothy 3:16-17

A religious person studies the word to prove himself; he does it to gain the approval of men. The goal of his studies is not to gain the approval of God by the life he lives; the goal is to gain the praises of men after he has preached. The religious person approaches the Word of God with a closed mind – he already knows. In order to break the spirit of religion, you must be teachable. Do not read into the scriptures. I have seen people read into the Word what they want so that they can prove their point. The scripture is not for private interpretation. You can imagine what would happen if we were all to have our own interpretations.

Start looking at the scriptures through new lenses and ask Holy Spirit to teach you. Most of what we believe is what has been handed down to us. We need to have our own conviction and move away from doing things simply because it is what we were told to do. What do *you* rely believe? What do *you* really know? *As soon as it was night, the brothers sent Paul and Silas away to Berea. On arriving there, they went to the Jewish synagogue. 11 Now the Bereans were of more noble character than the Thessalonians, for they received the message with great eagerness and examined the Scriptures every day to see if what Paul said was true.* Acts 17:10-11

These Bereans examined the scriptures that Paul and Silas taught. Today, the church has a spirit of lethargy and complacency, two elements that the spirit of religion is attracted to. A lazy Christian is a sure target for the spirit of religion. Break the spirit of laziness and start pursuing the Word of God as if your very life depended upon it. Job, during the entire period of his calamity declared in Job 23:12, "Neither have I gone back from the commandment of his lips; *I have esteemed the words of his mouth more than my necessary food.*"

You also must seek the whole counsel of God. A partial believer is still an unbeliever. A person should not pick out his favorite scriptures to obey and discard the not-so-favorable ones. Receive all of God's word and trust Holy Spirit's guide. He will teach you all things and lead you into all truths. The religious spirit opposes anything that is spirit-ordained. The gifts of the spirit are not allowed to flow and function in a religious atmosphere. To counter the works of religion, embrace the full gifts of God, Christ, and Holy Spirit in His church.

If you believe in Christ alone as your Savior and have not received the baptism of the Holy Spirit, simply ask The Father to baptize you. If you do not speak in tongues, simply ask your Heavenly Father to give you new tongues so that you can pray and worship Him in the spirit (Acts 2: 1-4). If you have been saved a long time ago but do not know if you have a spiritual gift or what your gift is, simply ask your Father to show you. As you serve in your local church, your spiritual leaders can help you to understand the works of the Spirit (1 Corinthians 12).

It is your responsibility to study the word. We are encouraged every day to study the word of God. (2 Timothy 2:15 KJV) However, this is only the first part of being teachable. The second part is where you apply the word to your life daily. Once again, the religious knows the word but seldom does the word. If he does obey the word at all, it is done only when convenient to him. To break this spirit you must obey the whole counsel of God. Make a decision to obey God's word in spite of the cost. Sometimes obedience can be lonely and painful but the rewards for obeying God far outweigh the initial discomfort. Just obey the word and leave everything else to Him who is able to keep you from falling.

Maintain Your Passion

The religious Laodicean church was a passionless church. They had programs but no power; they had rituals but no relationship. If you are going to influence and impact your world for God, you must develop a passionate relationship with God. Any lukewarmness will make you a target for the religious spirit. Begin to pray as Apostle Paul did: *"I want to know Christ and the power of his resurrection and the fellowship of sharing in his sufferings, becoming like him in his death, and so, somehow, to attain to the resurrection from the dead."* (Philippians 3: 10-11)

Christ must be your center; all people and things in your life must hinge on Christ alone. The verb used for *to know* is part of the verb *ginōskein*, which almost always indicates personal knowledge. It is not simply intellectual knowledge, the knowledge of certain facts or even principles. *It is the personal experience of another person.* The Old Testament uses *to know* of sexual intercourse. "Adam *knew* Eve his wife; and she conceived and bore Cain" (Genesis 4:1). In Hebrew the verb is *yada* and in Greek it is translated by *ginoskein*. This verb indicates the most intimate knowledge of another person. It is not Paul's aim *to know about Christ*, but to personally *know him* and it must be your aim also.

To stay free from the spirit of religion, relationship with Christ must be dynamic and refreshing. This can be obtained through prayer, worship (both private and public) and fellowship with other believers. Remember, do not get trapped by the religious prayer models that churches have been exposed to. For example, praying at the side of ones bed every morning at 5:00a.m can easily become a religious activity. Prayer is a lifestyle of communicating with God. It should not be limited to a certain time everyday or on special days or in a special place. We should pray without ceasing.

The same is true for worship. The person who worships God only on Sundays is a very religious person and in fact may not be worshiping God at all. To ward-off the spirit of religion a person must develop and practice a lifestyle of worship. Jesus had to explain to the Samaritian woman (who was steep in religion) the truth about worship. In John 4: 21-24. *Jesus declared, "Believe me, woman, a time is coming when you will worship the Father neither on this mountain nor in Jerusalem. 22 You Samaritans worship what you do not know; we worship what we do know, for salvation is from the Jews. 23 Yet a time is coming and has now come when the true worshipers will worship the Father in spirit and truth, for they are the kind of worshipers the Father seeks. 24 God is spirit, and his worshipers must worship in spirit and in truth."*

Worship is not something done in a special place or time; it is lifetime spent in total awe of God. Here are some additional scriptures that would encourage you to seek to know the only true God and Christ.

> *Now this is eternal life: that they may know you, the only true God, and Jesus Christ, whom you have sent.* John 17: 3

> *I keep asking that the God of our Lord Jesus Christ, the glorious Father, may give you the Spirit of wisdom and revelation, so that you may know him better.* Ephesians 1:17

> *At that time Jesus said, "I praise you, Father, Lord of heaven and earth, because you have hidden these things from the wise and learned, and revealed them to little children. 26 Yes,*

Father, for this was your good pleasure. 27 "All things have been committed to me by my Father. No one knows the Son except the Father, and no one knows the Father except the Son and those to whom the Son chooses to reveal him. Matthew 11:25-27

However, as it is written: "No eye has seen, no ear has heard, no mind has conceived what God has prepared for those who love him"— 10 but God has revealed it to us by his Spirit. The Spirit searches all things, even the deep things of God. 11 For who among men knows the thoughts of a man except the man's spirit within him? In the same way no one knows the thoughts of God except the Spirit of God. 1 Corinthians 2:9-12

Surely you have heard about the administration of God's grace that was given to me for you, 3 that is, the mystery made known to me by revelation, as I have already written briefly. 4 In reading this, then, you will be able to understand my insight into the mystery of Christ, 5 which was not made known to men in other generations as it has now been revealed by the Spirit to God's holy apostles and prophets. 1 Corinthians 2:9-12

To live a life worthy of God and please Him in every way, you must bear fruit in every good work and grow in the knowledge of God. (Colossians 1:

10) May you prosper in every good work and as a son of God bring freedom to others. Whom the Son has set free is free indeed.

To contact author
Please write:

Ann Marie Alman
4506 Church Avenue
Brooklyn NY 11210
or
E-mail: anncoolann@aol.com

For more exciting teaching
materials call:

Phone: 1-718-462-8389

Printed in the United States
202887BV00001B/1-180/P